Tables Are Turning:
German and Japanese Multinational Companies in the United States

PUBLICATION OF THE SCIENCE CENTER BERLIN
Volume 33

Editorial Board

International Institute of Management

Tables Are Turning: German and Japanese Multinational Companies in the United States

Anant R. Negandhi
University of Illinois at Urbana-Champaign

B. R. Baliga
Texas Tech University

Oelgeschlager, Gunn & Hain, Publishers, Inc.
Cambridge, Massachusetts

Verlag Anton Hain
Königstein/Ts.

658.16
N38t

International Standard Book Number: 0-89946-088-7 (U.S.A.)
3-445-02101-5 (Germany)

B4/

Library of Congress Catalog Card Number: 81-1445

Printed in West Germany

Library of Congress Cataloging in Publication Data

Negandhi, Anant R.
    Tables are turning.

    1. Corporations, German-United States — Management.   2. Corporation,
Japanese — United States — Management.   3. Underdeveloped areas — International business
enterprises — Management.   I. Baliga, B. R.   II. Title.
HD62.4.N44   658.1'6   81-1445
ISBN 0-89946-088-7

To Pia and Meghna

Contents

List of Figures

List of Tables

Foreword

The International Institute of Management's concern with the phenomenon of the multinational corporation (MNC) follows three streams.

1. Studies of the structure and dynamics of industries, concentrating on issues of growth on one hand and of stagnation on the other. Foreign direct investment—i.e., in international concerns—is one of the most explicit growth strategies. Thus, investigations have been undertaken to describe and explain the behavior of multinational corporations in this respect.
2. Studies of the participation of enterprises—national as well as multi- or transnational—in the realization of national industrial policies (structural, labor market, regional, etc.) when corporations act as government agents.
3. Studies of the managerial investment, market, and related behavior of MNCs. Multinational corporations were criticized publicly during the late 1960s and early 1970s for a number of reasons. Although the criticism did not discriminate between MNCs, it originated from dissatisfaction with U.S.-based multinationals. Once the scrutiny began, non-U.S.-based MNCs also were found to have failed in certain respects. For example, when Japanese MNCs, which were then quite new, tried to employ Japanese management practices, they malfunctioned in non-Japanese environments.

This volume continues a series of studies, made at the International Institute of Management of the Science Center Berlin under Professor Anant Negandhi's leadership, of managerial practices and corporate strategies of MNCs.* The Institute wants to express its sincere gratitude to Professors Negandhi and to Baliga for their deliberations into shedding light on one of our time's most debated institutions. No doubt, their study not only will contribute toward a better understanding of MNC behavior but also will lend realism and objectivity to the debate.

The Institute also wants to thank cosponsoring organizations for their confidence and support. Sincere thanks are expressed to the many, by necessity unknown, people who made the study possible by placing their time and experience at the researchers' disposal.

Walter H. Goldberg
Director, 1973–1979
International Institute of Management

---

*For example, see two books by Negandhi, *Modern Organizational Theory* (1973) and *Interorganizational Theory* (1980), both published by Kent State University Press; A.R. Negandhi and S.B. Prasad, *The Frightening Angels: A Study of U.S. Multinationals in Developing Countries* (Kent State University Press, 1975); and A.R. Negandhi and B.R. Baliga, *Quest for Survival and Growth: A Comparative Study of American, European, and Japanese Multinationals* (Praeger Publishers and Athenäum Verlag, 1979). Other publications will follow.

Preface

Tables Are Turning represents the changing organizational strategies, policies, and practices of German and Japanese multinational corporations (MNCs). This volume, based on intensive case studies of seventeen German subsidiaries and sixteen Japanese subsidiaries operating in the United States, portrays these changing patterns and indicates that the structures, strategies, policies, and practices of the MNCs appear to be converging. The implications of convergence are analyzed by comparing the policies and practices of German and Japanese MNCs in the United States with those in the six developing countries.

This book is the first of two volumes reporting the results of a large-scale study undertaken with 158 subsidiaries and 39 respective headquarters of American, British, German, Japanese, and Swedish multinational corporations.

The study was sponsored and supported by the International Institute of Management, Science Center Berlin, and the Institute of International Business at the Stockholm School of Economics. It was a collaborative effort, undertaken by six academic colleagues living and working on both sides of the Atlantic: Anant R. Negandhi (University of Illinois); Lars Otterbeck (Stockholm School of Economics); B.R. Baliga (Texas Tech University); Enders Edström and Gunnar Hedlund (Stockholm School of Economics); and Martin Welge (University of Hagen).

We are deeply indebted to the principal institution, the International Institute of Management, Science Center Berlin, for its generous financial and moral support of this study. We are also thankful to our present institutions, the University of Illinois at Urbana-Champaign and the University of Hagen, as well as our former institutions, the University of Cologne and the University of Wisconsin at Eau Claire, for their computer and typing support.

Many persons contributed generously to our efforts. These include: Professor Dr. Walter Goldberg, Senior Research Fellow and former Director of the International Institute of Management, Science Center Berlin, and Professor of Business Administration at the University of Gotenburg, Sweden. Dr. Goldberg, both as a director and a colleague, supported us immensely throughout this study, and his unfailing inspiration contributed substantially to the completion of this book.

My colleagues at the International Institute, Professors Bernhard Wilpert, George W. England, and the late Makoto Takamiya, provided considerable intellectual stimulation for the study, and we are grateful to all of them. We are also thankful to the director designate of the International Institute, Professor Dr. Bernhard Gahlen, for his continued support of this study.

Two graduate assistants, Mr. Prasad Vasireddi, at the International Institute of Management, and Mrs. Golpira Eshghi, at the University of Illinois, were extremely helpful during various phases of the study. Mrs. Carol Halliday and her colleagues at the Word Processing Center, at the University of Illinois, cheerfully typed the various drafts of the manuscript.

A number of executives from the multinational companies in various countries contributed generously of their time and thoughts, without which this study would not have been possible. Although their names must remain anonymous, we are nevertheless deeply indebted to them for their help.

Last, but not the least, to our families we owe a deep sense of gratitude for their moral support.

A.R.N.
B.R.B.

Chapter 1

A Challenge to American Business

This volume is concerned with the management orientations, strategies, policies, and practices of subsidiaries of the German and Japanese multinational corporations (MNCS) in the United States and management orientations and practices of American, European, and Japanese multinationals operating in six developing countries: Brazil, India, Malaysia, Peru, Singapore, and Thailand.

The main objectives of this comparative study of the three types of multinational corporations were to examine:

the similarities and differences in management orientations, strategies, policies, and practices of different types of multinational corporations in developed versus developing countries;

the impact of environmental factors (e.g., market and economic conditions, governmental policies and demands) on management strategies, policies, and practices;

the impact of management orientations, strategies, and policies on organizational efficiency and effectiveness.

To place our study in a proper perspective, it may be useful to outline the overall settings and assumptions underlying our endeavor and research approach.

2 /   *Tables Are Turning*

THE SETTINGS

Although American direct foreign investment represented 47.6 percent of the total foreign investments by all the countries, in 1976, it has been steadily declining since 1970. As can be seen from Table 1-1, the U.S. share of foreign investments declined from 53.8 percent in 1967, to 52.3 percent in 1971 to 47.6 percent in 1976, while West Germany's share increased from a mere 2.8 percent in 1967 to 4.6 percent in 1971 to 6.9 percent in 1976. During the same period, Japan increased its share from 1.4 percent to 2.8 percent and then to 6.7 percent.

Table 1-1. Foreign Direct Investment of Major Industrialized Countries, 1967 and 1976

	Billions of Dollars			Percentages		
	1967	1971	1976	1967	1971	1976
United States	56.6	82.8	137.2	53.8	52.3	47.6
United Kingdom	17.5	23.7	32.1	16.6	15.0	11.2
West Germany	3.0	7.3	19.9	2.8	4.6	6.9
Japan	1.5	4.4	19.4	1.4	2.8	6.7
Switzerland	5.0	9.5	18.6	4.8	6.0	6.5
France	6.0	7.3	11.9	5.7	4.6	4.1
Canada	3.7	6.5	11.1	3.5	4.1	3.9
Netherlands	2.2	4.0	9.8	2.1	2.5	3.4
Sweden	1.7	2.4	5.0	1.6	1.5	1.7
Belgium and Luxembourg	2.0	2.4	3.6	1.9	1.5	1.2
Italy	2.1	3.0	2.9	2.0	1.9	1.0
Total	101.3	153.3	271.5	96.2	96.8	94.2
All other (estimate)	4.0	5.1	16.8	3.8	3.2	5.8
Grand total	105.3	158.4	288.3	100.0	100.0	100.0

Source: United Nations, Centre on Transnational Corporation, *Transnational Corporations in World Development Re-examined* (New York; 1978).

A similar trend is also noticeable in the establishment of new subsidiaries overseas by American, European, and Japanese MNCs. For example, during 1971 American MNCs established 446 new subsidiaries overseas, while by 1975, the establishment of new subsidiaries declined by 63 percent, to a total of 204.[1]

In spite of the considerable lead that the American firms enjoyed before and immediately after World War II, the differences between large American and European enterprises are narrowing quickly; for example, Franko cites a major shift in international busines:

1. In 1959, an American company was the largest in the world, in 11 out of 13 major industries—namely, aerospace, automotive, chemicals,

electrical equipment, food products, paper, petroleum, phar-maceuticals, textiles, and commercial banking. By 1976, the United States was leading in only 7 out of 13. Three of the non-American leaders in 1976 were German, one was British-Dutch, one was British, and one was Japanese.

2. The number of U.S. companies among the world's top 12 declined in all industry groups except aerospace, between 1959 and 1976. Continental European companies increased their representatives among the top 12 in 9 out of 13 industries; the Japanese scored gains in 8.

3. Continental European companies scored particular gains in six industries: chemicals, automotive vehicles, primary metals, metal products, commercial banking, and pharmaceuticals. The number of the Continental European companies on the list of the world's top 12 in each industry equaled or exceeded the number of the U.S. companies in 1976.[2]

As Table 1-1 indicates, the Swiss, German, Japanese, and Dutch investment growth rates vastly exceeded those of the United States and the United Kingdom during the past decade. In addition, by 1971 the total sales of large European manufacturing companies outside their home countries exceeded the foreign sales of large U.S. industrial companies.[3]

A more aggressive posture of investment by the foreign multinationals can also be witnessed by examining the so-called reverse flow of investment — that is, the direct foreign investment in the United States by foreign firms. The growth of these investments has been staggering. For example, between 1975 and 1977 the number of foreign manufacturing firms in the United States roughly tripled and increased from 1246 firms in 1975 to 3433 firms in 1979.[4]

Among the ten leading foreign countries investing in the United States, West Germany and Japan recorded the highest growth. West German firms increased from 203 in 1974 to 710 in 1978, while during the same period Japanese firms increased from a mere 48 in 1976 to 203 in 1978.[5] The Japanese firms in particular have been very aggressive in increasing their share of direct foreign investment in the United States. Japanese private investment increased from $591 million in 1975 to $1178 million in 1976 to $1741 million in 1977.[6]

The declining status and share of U.S. private foreign investment can also be seen from the recent trends in voluntary disinvestment by U.S. firms. For example, the number of foreign divestments by the 500 largest U.S. multinationals grew from 50 in 1967 to 335 in 1975. During the years 1967 to 1975, the 180 largest U.S.-based multinationals added 4700 affiliates, while over 2400 were liquidated, sold, or nationalized. In 1971, there were 3.3 new investments for each disinvestment, and that ratio shrunk from 1.4 to 1.0 by 1975.[7] Disinvestments by European and Japanese multinational firms have also been increasing in recent years, although the ratio of new investments to disinvestments is still lower than that of the U.S. firms.[8]

REASONS FOR THE
NON-AMERICAN CHALLENGE

Besides the low start-up volume of foreign investment by the European and Japanese multinationals, the higher growth rate of these multinationals has been attributed to higher expenditure for research and developmental activities, resulting in improved capabilities for product and process innovations, narrowing of the so-called management and technological gaps between American and non-American firms, and better adaptability of non-American MNCs.[9].

It is now clear that Servan-Schreiber's *American Challenge*[10] not only failed to materialize but also was successful in creating *The European Revenge*[11] and what we will call The "Japanese Challenge."[12] In specific terms, as Franko writes, "By the 1970s, large non-American companies had learned how to systematically manage modern, multidivisional organizations—and had perhaps improved on U.S. practices by adopting more collegial less adversarial management styles."[13]

Besides improved capacities in product innovations and production processes, growth in productivity of manufacturing in Germany, France, and Japan outstripped those gains in the United States. Labor productivity in Japan doubled during the 1967–1977 decade, and that of Germany increased by 70 percent, compared with 27-percent increases in the United States (see Table 1–2).[14]

During the 1970s, the United States had the lowest rate of productivity growth of any major industrial nation. For example, in the private sector the growth rate dropped from 3 percent during the 1950s and 1960s to approximately 2 percent during the 1970–1977 period.[15]

This decrease in labor productivity has been attributed both to a lack of adequate capital investment and to a decrease in R&D expenditures. It is estimated that today the average U.S. plant is twenty years old; the average age of a plant in West Germany is twelve years, and in Japan, ten years.[16]

In recent years, U.S. R&D expenditures, in proportion to the gross national product (GNP), have been declining while those of Germany, Switzerland, and Japan are increasing. West German, Swiss, Dutch, and Japanese privately funded R&D expenditures, as a percentage of the GNP, have come to surpass those of the United States.[17] The close ties between government and business in Western Europe and Japan have been cited as instrumental in achieving higher growth rates for industrial enterprises in those countries.[18]

Table 1-2. International Indexes of Labor Productivity, 1960-1977 (Output Per Hour of Manufacturing Workers, 1967 = 100)

Year	United States	Japan	West Germany
1960	78.8	52.6	66.4
1961	80.6	59.3	70.0
1962	84.3	61.9	74.4
1963	90.1	67.1	78.4
1964	94.8	75.9	84.5
1965	98.1	79.1	90.4
1966	99.6	87.1	94.0
1967	100.0	100.0	100.0
1968	103.6	112.6	107.6
1969	105.0	130.0	113.8
1970	104.5	146.5	116.1
1971	110.3	150.5	121.4
1972	116.0	161.0	128.7
1973	119.0	179.0	136.6
1974	112.8	180.3	145.0
1975	116.3	172.4	150.4
1976	124.2	194.8	162.8
1977	126.9	206.6	169.6

Source: R. McConnel "Why Is U.S. Productivity Slowing Down?" *Harvard Business Review,* Vol. 57, No. 4 (March–April 1979): 36–62.

A number of scholars have also pinpointed the importance of management orientations, policies, and strategies, as well as flexibility in coping with ever-changing environments.[19] In recent years much has been said and written about the management orientations, strategies, policies, and practices of European and Japanese firms. Hardly a day goes by without some newspaper or popular weekly periodical covering success stories of these companies and pinpointing their unique management strategies and practices, although thus far such newspaper reportage, as well as academic studies, has been very selective and narrowly defined.[20] In particular, detailed and comparative perspectives are lacking to ascertain the relative strengths and weaknesses of the American, European, and Japanese approaches.

The main purpose of our study was to examine the similarities and differences among the American, German, and Japanese management orientations, strategies, policies, and practices. In so doing, we were able to shed some light on the impact of the environmental factors (e.g., market conditions, governmental regulations) on the management strategies and practices.

Chapters 2 through 4 report the results of two interrelated studies undertaken in the United States and the six developing countries.

In the remainder of this chapter, we will briefly outline the theoretical rationale for studying the strategies and practices of the multinational corporations; then we will provide some details about our own approach and methodology used in this study.

STRUCTURE FOLLOWS STRATEGY: CHANDLER'S THESIS

Utilizing the Product-Life-Cycle thesis and Chandler's theoretical paradigm that structure follows strategy,[21] the Harvard Multinational Project Group sought to understand the reasons for foreign direct investment overseas by the U.S. multinational companies and their strategies, structures, and processes in internationalizing the firms' operations.[22] In brief, the results of various studies undertaken with such theoretical thinking indicate that the firms' desire to retain control through wholly owned subsidiaries overseas is a function of certain contextual factors, such as size, level of diversification, the extent of R&D activities, advertising intensity, marketing strategies utilized, processes to reduce cost, desire and necessity to control the supply of raw material, and the firm's management ideologies or philosophies.[23] To put it simply, these researchers have shown that the thrust toward achieving economies of scale (or the so-called global rationalization criterion), along with the desire to establish control over the raw material supply, will lead to a wholly owned subsidiary option. Likewise, firms emphasizing product innovation will select wholly owned subsidiaries for controlling and coordinating their global operations.[24]

In tracing the evolution of the structural forms of an organization, the Harvard group indicated that the firm's structure will evolve from mere export or foreign departments to handle its overseas business to the formulation of an international division within the domestic organization to an international corporation structure — leading to a multinational concept with area and product concentration — to a matrix organizational form, and eventually to a transnational enterprise.

Using a similar theoretical rationale, both Franko and Yoshino predicted the same trend for the European and Japanese MNCs.[25] That is, the organizational structures of these MNCs have evolved from an export division to an international division to a separate international corporation, and finally to a divisionalized structure with product and area concentrations.

ASSUMPTIONS AND PREMISES

The logic of Chandler's thesis, structure follows strategy, has been validated through the various research studies undertaken with this theoretical paradigm, both at intranational and international levels.[26]

However, thus far the research studies based on Chandler's theoretical rationale have emphasized the internal aspects of organizational policy-making, and not enough attention is being paid to the external environmental forces impinging on the strategy–structure construct.

Second, the "rightness" of congruence between the firm's strategy and its structure is inferred through the economic performance criteria, although the linkage between strategy, structure, and performance has not yet been empirically verified.[27] It is conceivable, however, that a firm's economic and financial performance may be a function of market, economic, and political conditions rather than of the firm's strategy and structure.[28]

Given that most of the empirical work, done during the late 1960s and early 1970s by the Harvard group, was undertaken in the industrialized countries where free and competitive market conditions were prevalent and government interference was minimal, it was easier to overemphasize the internal aspects of organizations and underemphasize the macro external environmental conditions.

Since the 1973 oil crisis, economic and market conditions have changed drastically, both in the developed and in the developing countries. Government intervention and regulations that used to be the hallmark of centralized and developing economies have now become pervasive in industrialized countries as well.[29]

Given such changes in economic and political environments around the world, we were guided with the following assumptions in our study:

The strategies of the MNCs are influenced by the demands made by constituents in both host and home countries. Such demands are being made, not in the context of free economy market forces, but in terms of government-imposed controls on and regulatory measures for MNCs. On the basis of this premise, we hypothesized that the strategies of the MNCs should be in congruence with the policies and demands of the home and host countries.

To be effective in the varied environments of home and host countries (i.e., to agree with the varied demands and policies), the MNCs may have to devise different strategies for their home offices and their subsidiary operations. In other words, a master plan (e.g., the IBM and Coca Cola policy on 100-percent equity in all foreign operations) may become dysfunctional and nonoperational if the demands made by host countries are different.

Structures and processes of headquarters and subsidiaries must be consistent with the different strategies used by headquarters and subsidiaries to cope with the demands of the home and host country (environments).

The lack of congruence between the demands of the home and host countries and the strategies and structures of the headquarters and subsidiaries will be reflected in tensions and conflicts between headquarters and subsidiaries, between headquarters and host as well as home countries, and between subsidiaries and host countries.

Sample and Method

The U.S. study reported in this volume covered seventeen German subsidiaries and sixteen Japanese manufacturing subsidiaries operating in the United States. The study in the developing countries covered a total of 124 subsidiaries of American, European, and Japanese MNCs.

The rationale for comparing the German and the Japanese companies operating in the United States with those operating in the six developing countries was that such a comparison would allow us to examine the impact of a wide variety of environmental settings on management orientations, strategies, and practices.

It may be underscored, however, that we used somewhat different approaches in our studies. In the U.S. study, our focus was to examine the management strategies, policies, and practices, while in the study of the developing countries we were mainly interested in examining the nature and intensity of conflict and conflicting issues between the multinationals and the host countries. Only through the examination of these conflicts were we able to ascertain the specific management orientations, strategies, policies, and practices of the American, European, and Japanese MNCs. However, in spite of the different approaches, we believe that the results of the two different studies do provide some useful comparative insights into MNC practices in developed versus developing countries.

We conducted in-depth interviews with chief executive officers, top management representatives, or both, from all the firms that had agreed to participate in the study. In doing so, we used a forty-page, semistructured interview guide. The interviews lasted about four to eight hours on the average, and in most cases were held over luncheon or dinner. These mealtime sessions proved to be extremely valuable, as the executives tended to relax, and thus, in narrating episodes related to organizational functioning, they revealed subtle, although very significant, aspects of their operations. In the United States, top management executives were also asked to fill out a questionnaire that tapped some of the information sought in our interviews. About ninety-one usable questionnaires (forty-six from German and forty-five from Japanese subsidiaries) were returned.

In addition, we interviewed over fifty governmental officials and officials of Chambers of Commerce and other trade and professional organizations (including labor leaders) in the countries studied, both to solicit background information concerning the multinational operations and to obtain the officials' views and perspectives on various issues.

The characteristics of the companies studied are listed in Tables 1-3 and 1-4.

Table 1-3. Profiles of Companies Studied in the United States

	No. of German MNCs	No. of Japanese MNCs
Controlling ownership	17	16
Equity holding		
Wholly owned	17	16
Majority owned	0	1
No. of years operating in the U.S.		
Fewer than 5 years	0	3
5–15 years	5	13
More than 5 years	9	0
Degree of diversification		
Not diversified	0	10
Limited	8	6
Moderate	1	0
Extensive	8	0
Size of capital investment		
More than $7.5 million	14	0
$2–$7.5 million	3	6
Less than $2 million	0	10

Table 1-4. Profiles of Companies Studied in the Six Developing Countries

Controlling Ownership		Ratios of Equity		Size of Capital Investment	
American	= 54	Wholly owned	= 65	$4.99M–$3M	= 64
European	= 43	Majority owned	= 25	$2.99M–$2M	= 14
Japanese	= 27	Minority owned	= 24	$1.99M–$.5M	= 18
				Less than $.5M	= 9
		Not available	= 10	Not available	= 19

Diversification		Employment Size		Period of Operation	
More than 5 products	= 53	More than 1000	= 51	More than 15 years	= 76
2–5 products	= 31	999–400	= 23	6–14 years	= 35
Fewer than 2 products	= 36	399–100	= 31	Fewer than 6 years	= 10
		Fewer than 100	= 11		
Not available	= 4	Not available	= 8	Not available	= 3

Various details about the definitions and operationalization of variables are given in Appendix A. We have also attempted to provide a brief definition and operationalization of variables at the appropriate places in the text itself. The interview guides and the questionnaires used in the two studies appear as Appendixes B and C.

Organization of the Book

In the following chapter, we discuss the management orientations of German and Japanese subsidiaries operating in the United States. More specifically, the similarities and differences between these two sets of firms are highlighted with respect to their personnel policies, attitudes toward community, decisionmaking and information processing, time horizons, and attitude toward change. The chapter also covers the nature of headquarter–subsidiary relationships, control strategies, and integrating mechanisms of the Japanese and German subsidiaries.

In Chapter 3, we analyze the investment strategies, marketing orientations and practices, and pricing policies of the German and Japanese subsidiaries in the United States. The chapter also outlines the nature of attitude and response adopted by these firms toward public outcry on such issues as foreign imports, dumping practices, and preservation of the environment. Lastly, we explore the impact of their strategies and practices on the firms' efficiency and effectiveness.

To highlight the similarities and differences in the management orientations, strategies, policies, and practices of the European and Japanese companies in the industrialized versus developing countries, in Chapter 4 we discuss the results of our study conducted in the six developing countries. The chapter also provides data concerning subsidiaries of the U.S. multinational corporations.

In the last chapter, besides summarizing the overall results of these two studies, we explore the implications of our findings for the multinational corporations, for the home and host countries of the multinationals, and for academic researchers.

In presenting the results of both of these studies, we have refrained from using academic jargon, technical vocabulary, statistical analyses, and excessive tables. Instead, wherever possible, we have presented our findings in graphic form and have used the verbal expressions of the executives we interviewed. The technical aspects—such as definitions, conceptualization, and operationalization of variables—as well as the instruments used for these two studies are provided in the appendixes.

NOTES

1. J.P. Curhan, W.H. Davidson, and R. Suri, *Tracing the Multinationals* (Cambridge, Mass.: Ballinger Publishing Company, 1977).

2. L.G. Franko, "Multinationals: The End of U.S. Dominance," *Harvard Business Review*, Vol. 56, No. 2 (November–December 1978): 95–96.

3. Ibid., p. 96.

4. J. Arpan and D.D. Ricks, "Foreign Direct Investment in the U.S.," *Journal of International Business*, Vol. 10, No. 3 (Winter 1979): 85.

5. Ibid., p. 86.

6. W.K. Chung and G.G. Fauch, "Foreign Direct Investment in the United States," *Survey of Current Business* (August 1978): 46.

7. J. Boddewyn, "Disinvestment: Local vs. Foreign, and U.S. vs. European Approaches," *Management International*, Vol. 19, No. 1 (1979): 21.

8. Ibid., p. 21.

9. L.G. Franko, *The European Multinationals* (Stamford, Conn.: Greylock Publishers, 1976), especially ch. 7, pp. 2–22.

10. J.J. Servan-Schreiber, *The American Challenge* (New York: Athenaeum, 1968).

11. R. Heller and N. Willat, *The European Revenge* (New York: Charles Scribner's Sons, 1975).

12. H. Kahn, *The Emerging Japanese Superstate: Challenge and Response* (Englewood Cliffs, N.J.: Prentice-Hall, Inc., 1971).

13. Franko, "Multinationals," p. 98.

14. R. McConnel, "Why Is U.S. Productivity Slowing Down?" *Harvard Business Review*, Vol. 57, No. 4 (March–April 1978): 36–62.

15. F.L. Hartley, "World Trade in the 80's: Will We Be Competitive?" paper presented at 1980 World Trade Conference, Chicago, April 7, 1980.

16. Ibid.

17. Franko, "Multinationals," p. 98.

18. Ibid. Also see Y. Tsurumi, *The Japanese Are Coming: A Multinational Interaction of Firms and Politics,* (Cambridge, Mass.: Ballinger Publishing Company, 1976).

19. Franko, *The European Multinationals*. Also see A.R. Negandhi and B.R. Baliga, *Quest for Survival and Growth: A Comparative Study of American, European and Japanese Multinationals.* (New York: Praeger Publishers and Königstein, West Germany: Athenäum, 1979).

20. For example, see T.M. Rahan, "Europeans in America Practice Foreign Management," *Industry Week* (January 22, 1979): 64–67; J. Farley, "Winners and Losers in the Eighties," *World Business Weekly* (April 28, 1980): 5; and J.S. McClenahen, "Cultural Hybrids: Japanese Plants in the U.S.," *Industry Week* (February 19, 1979): 73–75.

21. A. Chandler, *Strategy and Structure* (Cambridge, Mass.: MIT Press, 1962).

22. R. Vernon, *Sovereignty at Bay: The Mutlinational Spread of U.S. Enterprises* (New York: Basic Books, Inc., 1971). Also see John Stopford and L.T. Wells, *Managing the Multinational Enterprise — Organization of the Firm and Ownership of the Subsidiaries* (New York: Basic Books, Inc., 1972).

23. Ibid., ch. 10, pp. 144–149.

24. Ibid.

25. Franko, *The European Multinationals*.

26. For example, see Stopford and Wells, *Managing the Multinational Enterprise;* Franko, *The European Multinationals;* Yoshino, *Japan's Multinational Enterprises;* G.P. Dyas and H.T. Thanheiser, *The Emerging European Enterprise* (London: Macmillan, Ltd., 1976); R.R. Rumlet, *Strategy, Structure and Economic Performance* (Boston: Division of Research, Harvard Business School, 1974).

27. J.R. Galbraith and D.A. Nathansan, *Strategy Implementation: The Role of Structure and Process* (St. Paul, Minn.: West Publishing Company, 1978), p. 47.

28. Joe Bain, *Industrial Organization* (New York: John Wiley and Sons, 1958).

29. "Key Concerns for MNCs During the Year Ahead Make for a Grim 1980," *Business International* (January 4, 1980): 1–8.

Chapter 2

Management Orientation of the German and Japanese Subsidiaries

In this chapter we examine the management orientation of German and Japanese subsidiaries operating in the United States. In so doing, we discuss the similarities and differences in their personnel policies, attitudes toward community, decisionmaking and information-sharing orientation, attitude toward change (reactivity), and time orientations.[1] First, we discuss the overall management orientation of the Japanese multinationals, and then examine the specific aspects of their management orientation in detail.

MANAGEMENT STYLES

The Japanese Orientation

The overall Japanese management orientation is summed up comprehensively in "the cyle of goodness" theme propounded by the president of YKK (the world's largest manufacturer of zippers) to guide its operations. He states:

I firmly believe in the spirit of social service. Wages alone are not sufficient to assure our employees of a stable life and a rising standard of living. For this reason, we return to them a large share of the fruits of their labor, so that they may also

13

participate in capital accumulation and share in the profits of the firm. Each employee, depending upon his means, deposits with the company at least 10 percent of his wages and monthly allowances, and 50 percent of his bonus; the company, in turn, pays interest on these savings. Moreover, as this increases capital, the employees benefit further as stockholders in the firm. It is said that "the accumulation" of savings distinguishes man from animals. Yet, if the receipts of a day are spent within that day, there can be no such cycle of saving.

The savings of all YKK employees are used to improve production facilities, and contribute directly to the prosperity of the firm. Superior production facilities improve the quality of the goods produced. Lower prices increase demand. And both factors contribute to the prosperity of other industries that use our products.

As society prospers, the need for raw materials and machinery of all sorts increases, and the benefits of this cycle spread not just to this firm, but to all related industries. Thus the savings of our employees, by enhancing the prosperity of the firm, are returned to them as dividends that enrich their lives. This results in increased savings which further advance the firm. Higher income means higher tax payments, and higher tax payments enrich the lives of every citizen.

In this manner, business income directly affects the prosperity of society for businesses are not mere seekers after profit, but vital instruments for the improvement of society.

This cycle enriches our free society and contributes to the happiness of those who work within it. The perpetual prosperity for all.

This is the cycle of goodness.[2]

That this view is not unique can be ascertained from the orientation of some of the largest and most successful Japanese firms. For instance, Toyota's slogan is: "Harmony with communities in partner countries." The management orientation of Matsushita (one of the most profitable of all Japanese companies) is expressed in the following words:

Service, not profit, is the objective. Profit is not what we can earn — it is given to Matsushita in appreciation of its services. If the company fails to make its profit, it has committed a social blunder or sin, according to our philosophy. The society to which Matsushita belongs entrusts it with capital and manpower for Matsushita to get results. Profit is the appreciation of society, the reward to Matsushita for what it has done.[3]

Thus the "oneness" of the corporation and the community and the high concern for the employees are considerably stressed in the overall management philosophy.[4] Indeed, such philosophical overtones can be found in some of the manuals of the U.S. companies as well. How far such lofty overtones on the philosophies or policies of the companies are translated into actual practices is the real question that we attempted to investigate.

The Personnel Orientation

Nakane stated that the Japanese "companies hire potential not skills."[5] If employees are viewed as a reservoir of skills, they can also be viewed as dispensable as skill requirements change in the organization as a result of changes in technology or changes in output. In such an orientation, layoffs and dismissals of employees are an essential and integral part of the industrial system with management possessing the right to determine which skills are desirable at a particular time. In such an industrial system, management has a greater level of authority and influence, and the only way for employees to achieve their desires is to take away some of this influence and authority from management through bargaining and negotiating. This confrontational approach is, of course, the hallmark of the industrial relations system in the West, especially in the United States, which has translated itself in the persistent refusal of American managers to even consider involving labor in managerial decisions. Workers have also generally resisted moves that were perceived by them as being designed to co-opt them and reducing their bargaining power. Representatives of U.S. labor have reacted in a similar manner.

On the other hand, when Japanese employers hire "potential" rather than skills there is little likelihood of classifying an employee as simply a source of particular skills. Serious attempts are being made to foster an attitude of being *in* a company rather than *with* a company. A constant problem confronting many industrialized nations in the West has been that of alienation from work[6] which has resulted in low productivity, poor quality of output, high turnover, and absenteeism.[7] Japanese organizations, both in Japan and in their subsidiaries in the United States, do not face such problems.[8] Labor turnover and absenteeism in Japanese subsidiaries in the United States, for example, are approximately 50 percent below the rates for comparable U.S. firms, despite the fact that Japanese managers have minor communication and sociocultural problems.[9] The extent to which Japanese management is concerned with the welfare of its employees is illustrated in the following representative cases gathered during our interviews with the executives of Japanese subsidiaries in the United States:

The Blue-Collar Case

A major Japanese multinational had just acquired a unit of a large American multinational company. Prior to the Japanese acquisition, the company had received stepchild treatment from the American parent. For example, the roof of the plant leaked profusely, and the plant floor was in shambles.

Immediately upon takeover, Japanese management held a meeting with all plant employees, sought their views on employee welfare, and proceeded to fix the roof and the floor. As a measure of good faith, they retained local (American) management even though the company was losing money. Within a few months, morale at the plant zoomed, and the company was well on its way to a record year despite a deepening recession. Workers at the plant interviewed were very enthusiastic about the developments and they seemed determined to work for establishing a strong position within the industry.

The White-Collar Case

A middle-level manager of a Japanese subsidiary dismissed an American executive who had not performed well. When the Japanese president of the subsidiary learned about it, he immediately summoned the middle-level manager and requested that he recall the fired executive, discuss with him the problems he had in performing his job satisfactorily, and if necessary, offer him another position more compatible with his abilities. This was done and the executive turned out to be an excellent performer in his new role, thus confirming the perspective that potential matters more than skills.

It must be emphasized that although these cases were representative of the Japanese orientation toward their employees, there were also exceptions. A classic exception was that of a unit located in the industrial belt around Chicago that had significant turnover and absenteeism. The executive interviewed cited the U.S. welfare system as a main cause of high turnover and absenteeism in this plant. In addition, the skill levels required of the employees were fairly low and equivalent (and easier) jobs could be found in the vicinity without too much trouble. The unit was the poorest performer of four similar subsidiaries in the United States.

Critics of Japanese practices have, however, asserted that the personal touch is just a "trick of the manager and that management promotes such a relationship with its employees, not out of their inherent goodness, but to keep the unions out." George Collins, leader of the International Union of Electrical, Radio, and Machine Workers, pointed out that it was union pressure that resulted in higher wages and benefits at the Sony San Diego plant and not the benevolence of Sony.[10] On the other side of the Atlantic, in a YKK plant in Italy, workers struck for eighteen months complaining about the hard-driving ten-man Japanese management team. Although the Japanese managers, to demonstrate their corporate loyalty, attempted to man the machines themselves, a labor magistrate found the company guilty of "anti-union activity" and ordered the managers to keep away from the production line during the strike.[11]

If the record of Japanese corporations in handling their employees in the developing countries is examined, a measure of truth in the criticism voiced above can be discerned. The treatment of their employees in the developing countries was less than humanistic and generated considerable conflict.[12] This situation could be interpreted as managerial adjustment to the availability of personnel. If the required workers are available with minimum trouble (as in the developing countries), Japanese managers appear to be willing to deemphasize the "personal touch" in their orientation toward their employees, whereas in the American labor market Japanese management apparently considered the personal touch orientation a sound business approach.

Notwithstanding such criticism and problems, our intensive interviews with the employees of Japanese subsidiaries in the United States revealed considerable employee satisfaction and appreciation of Japanese management practices, especially with respect to job rotation, lack of status differentials, and management's concern for the employees. The concept of recruiting personnel for their potential and not for their skills, especially at the white-collar level, requires some form of job rotation. Understaffing is also consciously maintained to facilitate such job rotation practices. Employees are expected to show initiative and are encouraged to accept responsibility. Initially, this *nondirective* form of management caused problems in managing U.S. subsidiaries, and it also led to complaints such as "we don't have enough responsibility" from American employees. Once employees assume responsibility on their own initiative, however, content with work becomes a strong motivator.

Japanese subsidiaries deemphasized status differentials. Executives and operatives generally worked in the same physical space—private offices were a rarity. As Clark puts it, "rank (status) is reflected in ritualistic behavior not in substantive issues."[13] Clark's observations were related to Japanese organizations operating in Japan. Our interviews of executives in Japanese subsidiaries in the United States indicated that even the ritualistic component of status was not present. Such deemphasis in status leads to an identification with the organization and has had considerable impact on information dissemination and decisionmaking. For example, William Nelson, Vice-President of a Japanese subsidiary in Wisconsin, Kikkoman Foods, appreciating the human aspect of Japanese management practices, said: "It's more people-oriented than any other plant I've ever worked with."[14]

Similarly, a senior executive at the Sony plant in San Diego, California, asserted:

> Japanese management tries to deal with the workers with a more personal touch. We try to be close to our workers. We have company outings to try to be more intimate. Our people all wear the same blue jacket. We have no class feelings.[15]

The German Orientation

Compared to the Japanese subsidiaries, status differentials were very visible in German subsidiaries; it also appeared that the role of status found in organizations in Germany was transferred across the Atlantic. Status symbols were reflected in the reserved parking spots, the size and location of private offices, and the critical gatekeeper function played by the executives' assistants and secretaries.[16] Such a gatekeeper function was rarely witnessed in Japanese subsidiaries. The personnel orientation practices in the German subsidiaries seemed to strike a balance between the "human relations" approach and the need for structure.

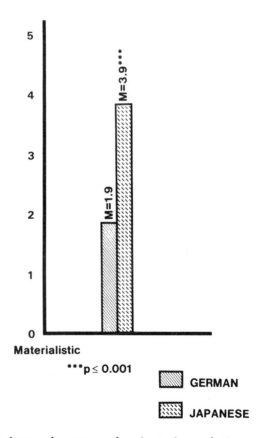

HUMANISTIC

Materialistic

***$p \leq 0.001$

GERMAN

JAPANESE

Figure 2-1a. Comparison of personnel orientation of German and Japanese subsidiaries in the United States.

Figure 2-1a shows the differences between the Japanese and German subsidiaries in their overall personnel orientation. As can easily be seen from this figure, the Japanese orientation seems to be considerably more "humanistic" than that of the German subsidiaries. Overall, Japanese subsidiaries appear to show more concern for their employees, for example, dissimenating information more widely across the various levels of hierarchy than the German subsidiaries in the United States.

Our analyses of various efficiency and effectiveness criteria, however, such as return on investment, return on sales, or overall efficiency in terms of input–output ratios, did not reveal significant differences between them. In other words, the greater concern of the Japanese subsidiaries for their employees, as well as their community, was not translated into higher performance and productivity by the employees. This lack of significant difference between the Japanese and German subsidiaries may be because the German companies operating in the United States employ a very high proportion of professional persons, such as engineers, system analysts, and scientists.[17] It has been shown that the job involvement, satisfaction, and performance of professional employees are more a function of professional pride and challenge than specific "soft" practices, such as a human relations approach, used by most organizations.[18]

In the long run, however, the impact of management concern toward employees and community may be considerable in terms of organizational survival and growth.[19] Thus, we will discuss in detail the subtle differences between Japanese and German subsidiaries with respect to their attitudes toward community, information sharing and decisionmaking, and response to changing environments and time orientations.

The Community Orientation

The role of business and its relation to society is increasingly coming under close scrutiny.[20] Not too long ago, the interrelationships between society and business were analyzed predominantly in economic terms; today, however, various interest groups in society are analyzing the role of the corporation from different perspectives: as a provider of goods and services; as an exploiter; and as a ravager of the environment. As a consequence, establishing legitimacy has become an increasingly difficult task for most corporations. This issue is even more complex for subsidiaries of MNCs. Xenophobic tendencies are invariably present under the surface, and even minor problems can cause considerable headaches for foreign companies in the host country. A corporation that is sensitive and reacts skillfully to the fears and aspirations of the community in which it is operating may have a better chance of attaining long-term effectiveness.

As shown in Figure 2-1b, Japanese subsidiaries appear to show a significantly higher level of community concern as compared to German

HIGH CONCERN

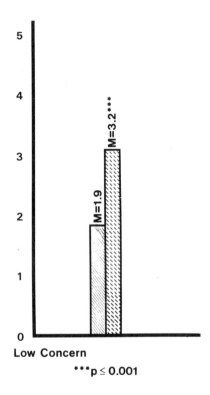

***p ≤ 0.001

Figure 2-1b. Comparison of community orientation of German and Japanese subsidiaries in the United States.

subsidiaries. In fact, a number of Japanese subsidiaries we interviewed have a deliberate policy of seeking information from key and influential decisionmakers in the host environment, and questions such as "what projects would best benefit the local economy, and what are the needs of the specific communities" were jointly discussed with community leaders.[21] Special mention should be made of the fact that the company shared these guidelines with its labor union and obtained its understanding, which resulted in considerable labor and management agreement on many issues.

The Mitsugoro project in Indonesia, a joint venture of Mitsui, and the agricultural cooperative Kosgoro, are excellent examples of this concept being translated into practice.[22] In the United States, Japanese subsidiaries, for example, have contributed substantially to the U.S. Olympic Committee, universities such as MIT, and to innumerable causes at the local level. Japanese companies have also been extremely careful not to exhibit their Japaneseness whenever it aroused negative emotional reactions in the immediate community. For example, a Japanese subsidiary in an American midwestern state did not display the Japanese national flag, even on ceremonial occasions, when the company found out that such display aroused negative feelings in the community because the residents had been heavily involved in operations in the Japanese theatre during World War II.

German subsidiary executives, by contrast, seemed to feel that playing the "good corporate citizen role" was sufficient to establish legitimacy, and they made little or no effort to become seriously involved with the immediate community in which they operated. It is true, however, that German firms were less likely to be singled out as "alien" operations, and therefore they had a lesser need to justify their operations.

The Information and Decisionmaking Orientation

Japanese companies practiced a more open and collegial orientation toward information sharing and decisionmaking, which was characterized by:

Deliberate action to seek inputs from all personnel who were either familiar with the subject under discussion or who would be affected by the decision.

Information pertaining to organizational functioning being made widely available to members of the organization. Most of the Japanese companies we visited had a "conference room" with visual displays pertaining to production, sales, absenteeism, turnover, productivity, equipment utilization, and so on.

Deemphasizing status differences and the diffuse nature of authority relations, as discussed earlier, were very conducive to this open orientation. Inputs and criticisms in most cases were accepted professionally and were rarely conceived as personal criticism. The collegial principle of decision-making was highly valued, and discussions invariably continued until a consensus was reached. Many scholars who have studied Japanese systems have argued that if a single factor has to be isolated to explain Japan's managerial and economic success, it would be the prevalence of an open and collegial decisionmaking approach, commonly labeled the "Ringi system."[23] A related aspect of this system, which has not been commonly discussed, is the role of the organizational leaders. Organizational leaders in Japanese organizations generally adopt nonassertive roles, but they are actively involved in formulating the conclusion of decisions.[24] Our results, shown in Figure 2–2a, confirm some of the commonly held views on Japanese and German orientation. As is evident, the facilitator role of

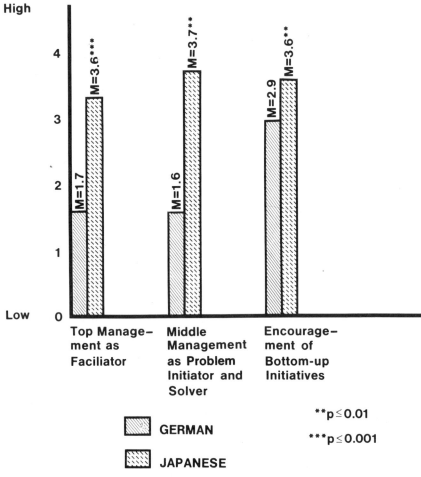

Figure 2–2a. Comparison of the roles of management personnel in German and Japanese subsidiaries in the United States.

Japanese top management is clearly highlighted. A number of middle-management personnel interviewed echoed similar views as those expressed by an American executive in a Japanese subsidiary:

> We are pretty much free to do whatever we like in terms of getting the job done. They do not ask us to do this or that; they welcome suggestions and listen very carefully to what we say. We feel free to disagree with them and they never hold it against us. When I was with an American company I always had to be careful with what I said lest I offend the boss. Here, if my idea is good it is always accepted.

In contrast, the top management decisionmaking orientation in German subsidiaries was relatively more autocratic. Top management invariably made the decisions in relative isolation, which were then passed down for implementation.

Figure 2–2a also indicates that the Japanese subsidiaries utilize middle management as problem initiators and problem solvers more frequently than the German subsidiaries. In the German subsidiaries, the role commonly played by middle management was that of a controller. They were expected to monitor the implementation of the decisions made by top management and report variations to top management for corrective action. Only in relatively rare instances did middle management have the authority to initiate action, and it was generally limited to the production function.

Figure 2–2a also indicates a relatively higher level of "bottom-up" initiatives encouraged by Japanese top management. Such practices have particularly important implications in the context of U.S. subsidiary operations. For example, Yoshino[25] has argued that the transfer of the Ringi system to the subsidiaries would create problems for both the Japanese and the non-Japanese employees, as the cultural context necessary for successful operation of the Ringi system (face-to-face interaction; recognition of subtle communication signals, etc., formed through a relatively long and intimate socialization process) would be absent. Interestingly enough, Clark, although confirming the presence of "a decisionmaking through consensus" mode in Japanese companies in Japan, compared the Ringi system to the Western (Anglo-Saxon) modes of decisionmaking in this way:

> (Western) . . . decisionmaking is presented as individualistic until adversity proves it collective. In Japan it is presented as collective until it is worth someone's while to claim a decision as his own.[26]

Pascale,[27] in a study of decisionmaking in Japanese subsidiaries in the United States, found very little evidence of the Ringi system being used. In fact, he found the decisionmaking modes to be very similar to those of the American firms, although he did find that Japanese subsidiaries with a significant proportion of expatriates relied more heavily on an "informal" communication style than those with a smaller percentage of Japanese nationals.

As discussed above, our results indicate that the Ringi system has been replaced by a "collegial system" of information sharing and decisionmaking in Japanese subsidiaries in the United States. The manner in which such a system functions is best explained by a senior American executive of a company acquired by a Japanese multinational:

> For the first few days it was a very strange experience. I was not very sure as to what was to be done and what I was supposed to be doing. I kept asking my

Japanese boss and he would reply: "Do whatever you think is necessary." Gradually I found myself defining my job. It was a great feeling. We (other senior executives) would talk about what we wanted to do and they (Japanese executives) would listen. They hardly disagreed and suggestions were basically guided toward making sure that all activities were coordinated. It's been five years now since they took over and each day I am enjoying my job more.

Similar sentiments across various organizational levels have been reported by other researchers.[28]

In contrast to the collegial system employed by Japanese subsidiaries in the United States, German subsidiaries follow a system very similar to that suggested by traditional management models,[29] in which the decision-making authority is clearly defined for most, if not all, positions within the organizations. Division of responsibility, rather than being unitary, is shared, however; that is, management is invariably collective, from the top-level boards of management down to the operating level, where, for example, a product division can be headed by two managers—one sales and the other technical.[30] Information flows within the organization are restricted to personnel who "have a need to know." It is also stressed that the appropriate channels should be followed, which are either indicated in organizational manuals or implicitly defined in job descriptions.

Our interviews gave us numerous opportunities to observe the handling of information. Interviews with Japanese executives were often interrupted by phone calls and messages that emanated from within and outside the organization—discussions were open and animated. Other executives and personnel felt free to walk in and out of the office and contribute to the interviews. For the German subsidiaries, however, interviews took place in an atmosphere of relative privacy.

The Reactivity and Time Orientation

These factors are concerned with determining whether or not a company adopts a long-term orientation for its operations, and the extent to which it feels compelled to react rapidly to disturbances in the environment. It could also be hypothesized that if the company adopts a long-term perspective, it would be more deliberate in responding to disturbances in the environment. As can be seen from Figure 2–2b, both Japanese and German subsidiaries operating in the United States maintain a fairly long-term perspective for their operations; actually, there is no significant difference between them. This observation conforms with the conclusions reached by Vogel[31] for Japanese multinationals and Franko[32] for European multinationals. This long-term orientation is well expressed by the General Manager of the San Diego Sony plant, Mr. Masayushi Morimoto: "We do not necessarily look for a quick payoff. . ."[33]

TIME

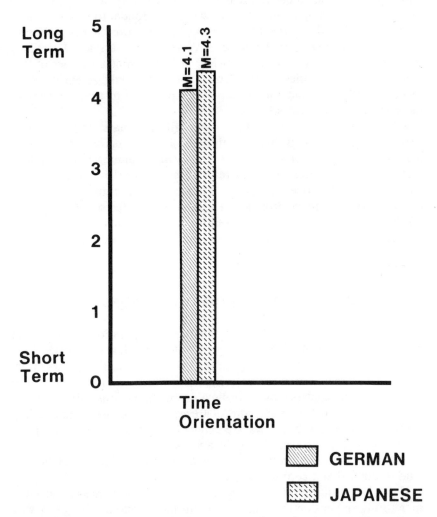

Figure 2–2b. Comparison of the time orientation of German and Japanese subsidiaries in the United States.

Achieving market stabilitity and building a solid employee relations foundation are conceived as having at least as high a priority as profits in the initial years.[34] Both Japanese and German subsidiaries were also very deliberate in reacting to disturbances in the environment, with the Japanese being more cautious or slower. For example, it is common knowledge that despite the sustained appreciation of the yen vis-à-vis the dollar and a growing nationalistic and protectionistic sentiment now prevalent in the United States, Japanese auto-makers have adopted a wait-and-see attitude. Apparently, they wish to determine the success of the Volvo and VW operations prior to making an investment decision.[35] Honda, too, waited for an interminable length of time before setting up a motorcycle assembly plant near Columbus, Ohio.[36] Japanese T.V. manufacturers acted similarly, waiting until a crisis point was reached before buying a number of T.V. manufacturing facilities in the United States.[37] Only recently, Nissan Motor, another big automobile exporter, consented to start an assembly plant in the United States.[38]

Kikkoman Shoyu Co., Ltd., spent fifteen years establishing its stronghold in the U.S. market through imports before setting up a manufacturing plant in Wisconsin.[39] Policy and planning models indicate that organizations must plan to react to changes in the environment.[40] Although this objective is laudable, it appears that a number of organizations overreacted to environmental stimuli and suffered drastically as a result. For this reason, apparently both German and Japanese managements are now reacting more cautiously to sudden shifts in the environments.

HEADQUARTER–SUBSIDIARY RELATIONS

Given the nature of the multinational corporation, control is the basic problem confronting the managers of the individual enterprises. Many organizational theorists have argued that as an organization grows in size, there is an increased need for differentiation, which, in turn, creates a need for integration, control, and coordination of the various subunits.[41] The problems of coordination and control are especially acute for multinational corporations. The subsidiaries are generally scattered around the globe, operating in varying degrees of dynamic and hostile environments. The need for global rationalization for many MNCs further intensifies the problems of control and coordination.

Headquarter–subsidiary relationships denote the processes employed for monitoring and evaluating subsidiary performance and the degree to which decisions are delegated to subsidiary levels. Significant delegation and informal monitoring and evaluation mechanisms constitute loose coupling between headquarters and the subsidiaries, while little delegation with formal monitoring and evaluation mechanisms constitute tight coupling. It must be emphasized that it is very unlikely that all aspects of an organization's operations will be either tightly or loosely coupled — for tight or loose coupling refers to the ideal or pure types.[42] It is possible, however, to identify the organizations as being more or less tightly coupled in an overall sense.

In order to determine the tightness of coupling, we initially asked the subsidiary management what they perceived as their level of influence versus the influence of headquarters on a series of decisions, such as investment decisions, advertising and promotion decisions, and appointment of the chief executive for the subsidiary operation. These decisions were then identified as either strategic or routine. An overall delegation index was then computed with strategic decisions given three times more weight than routine decisions. The weighting factor was chosen to reflect the approximate ratio of time for the feedback of strategic decisions as compared to routine decisions. Figures 2-3 and 2-4 present the findings for the delegation index and the extent of delegation along a set of decisions for the

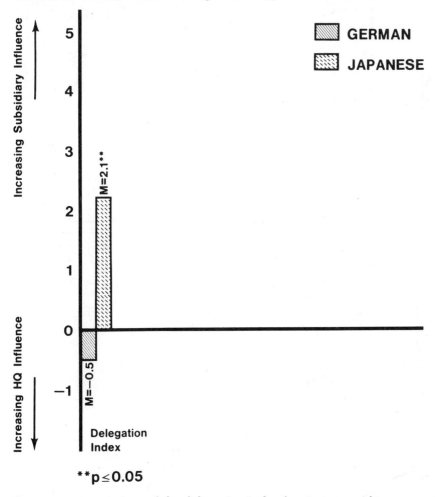

Figure 2-3. Comparison of the delegation index for German and Japanese subsidiaries.

German and Japanese subsidiaries, respectively. From these figures it is clear that the relative level of delegation for Japanese subsidiaries is higher than for German subsidiaries, although there was fairly extensive variation among each of them.

Ouchi[43] identified two types of control mechanisms:

Behavior control
Output control

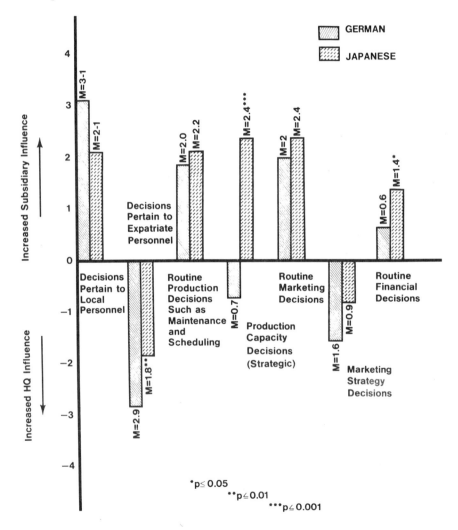

Figure 2-4. Comparison of the extent of delegation provided to German and Japanese subsidiary managements.

In order to exercise behavior control, the organization needs to have some agreement about the means–end relationship. Output control is generally the preferred mode of control if means–end relationships are unknown but reliable, and valid output measures are available. It is interesting to note from Figure 2–4 that there is essentially no difference between German and Japanese subsidiaries with regard to decisions about local personnel. Apparently, headquarters are willing to acknowledge that their knowledge of labor conditions in the host country is limited as compared to that of the subsidiary management, and hence, delegation is advisable. For decisions concerning expatriate personnel, headquarters have considerable influence, although Japanese subsidiary managers have more influence than their German counterparts. This difference is consistent in that the expatriate managerial personnel are significant links in the control mechanisms employed by their headquarters.[44]

Figure 2–4 also shows that routine production decisions and routine marketing decisions are delegated to subsidiary management, and that there is essentially no significant difference between the German and Japanese subsidiaries. The degree of delegation is probably fairly low when compared to the domestic divisions of corporations. A partial explanation probably lies in the fact that despite the acknowledgement of headquarters of a less than perfect understanding of the environment, of the subsidiary, the need for a global rationalization dictates lesser delegation of authority at the subsidiary level. This interpretation is underscored when examining production capacity decisions. We note that there is a significant difference between German and Japanese subsidiaries with Japanese subsidiaries having a much greater degree of delegation. German subsidiaries in the United States are basically involved in technologically sophisticated and capital-intensive operations, whereas Japanese subsidiaries are involved in less sophisticated, less capital-intensive, and smaller operations. As a result, German multinational systems are under a greater degree of pressure to rationalize their operations on a global basis.

It is interesting to note that delegation for strategic marketing decisions was also limited, both in German and Japanese subsidiaries. Greater efforts seem to be directed toward standardizing marketing programs internationally.[45] The large size and homogeneity of the U.S. market makes such standardization worthwhile. Standardization was also aided by the fact that many of the products or services offered by the subsidiaries in the United States were well established, requiring little or no consumer eduction. The need to rationalize production on a global scale also generated additional pressure on rationalizing marketing operations along similar lines. Franko[46] found that European subsidiaries operating in the United States had less flexibility (i.e., lesser delegation) in market policies as compared with subsidiaries of U.S. companies operating in Europe, although the difference was not as great as anticipated.

This limited delegation of strategic marketing decisions has posed problems for Japanese firms such as Sony, operating in the large U.S. consumer market. Limited delegation of marketing decisions to subsidiary management prevented a rapid reaction to retail price maintenance. From this indicator as well as others shown in Figure 2–4, it appears that the management at headquarters is still relatively unwilling to recognize the differences in environmental conditions in the host countries and their impact on subsidiary operations.[47]

Figure 2–4 also shows that financial decisions are more centralized. It is to be expected that in an MNC system with numerous subsidiaries, finance would clearly be a highly centralized function. Practically all the subsidiaries studied had a functional form of organizational structure, however. It has been argued that functional specialization leads to less emphasis on financial management; for example, capital expenditure decisions become subsumed under decisions to expand production capacity, and so on. It appears to us that the slightly greater level of delegation for financial decisions that the Japanese subsidiaries have is more a function of their size than anything else. The monetary sums involved for the Japanese subsidiaries are unlikely to be as high as those for the German subsidiaries, and hence, headquarters can afford to give greater delegation to the subsidiary management. An alternative explanation is suggested by the closer relationship of Japanese organizations to the banking system. Owing to the closer relationships between banks and headquarters, zones of authority within which the subsidiaries (of the bank and the corporation) can function in a relatively autonomous manner are easier to establish.[48]

STRATEGIES OF CONTROL

In the previous section, we discussed our findings about decision-making authority in the German and Japanese subsidiaries. In this section, we discuss our findings about the strategies of control employed by German and Japanese corporations.

Usually, two modes of control are used in complex organizations:
The bureaucratic mode
The personal mode[49]

The bureaucratic mode is characterized by a reliance on formal reports, rules, regulations, procedures, and so on, all of which serve to delimit authority; that is, zones of authority are created for the various positions in the organizaton. In the personal mode headquarters exercise control by placing a number of trustworthy personnel (from the headquarters) in key positions in the subsidiary.

Data were gathered from the subsidiaries studied on the frequency with which formal reports in each of the functional areas of business were required by corporate headquarters. Figure 2–5 presents the findings. As is evident, there were no substantial differences between the German and Japanese subsidiaries in the number of financial, marketing, and performance appraisal reports required. The only difference that emerged concerned production reports, which can be easily explained by the fact that the German operations were considerably larger in size and, as explained in the previous section, German MNCs made considerable efforts to rationalize their operations on a global basis. The Japanese plants, in contrast, were relatively small; they produced almost exclusively for local consumption. Our study also indicated an additional reason for the smaller emphasis on production reports by the Japanese corporation. As is discussed in the following chapter, a number of Japanese subsidiaries operating in the United States used equipment, semifinished goods, and in some cases even raw materials, furnished by the parent companies. As corporate headquarters had information about these shipments, they were able to make a fairly accurate assessment of production operations in the subsidiary.

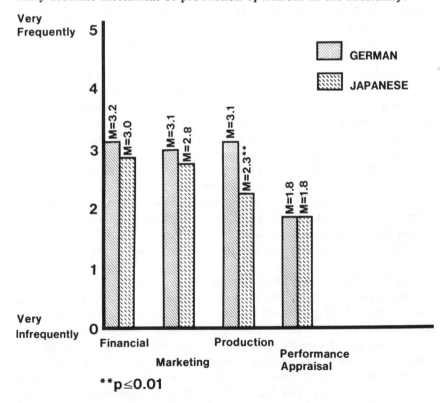

Figure 2–5. Comparison of reporting requirements for German and Japanese subsidiaries.

A somewhat surprising finding was the relatively low reporting requirement for performance appraisal. Unfortunately, we did not obtain this information separately for managerial personnel and operatives; what is presented is thus a mean response. An idea of the managerial performance appraisal could be inferred, however, by examining the delegation accorded to the subsidiary management for local personnel decisions. As reported in the previous section, both German and Japanese subsidiary managers had a great deal of autonomy in hiring local personnel. In congruence with this level of autonomy, the management at headquarters apparently felt it was unnecessary to obtain formal reports, the management at headquarters was in intimate contact with the managerial personnel—especially expatriates—on a day-to-day basis. In addition, a measure of their performance could be ascertained from the reports furnished by other functional areas.

Although there were few differences in the financial reporting requirements, except what could be explained by technology and size, there were substantial differences in the use of rules and regulations (extent of formalization) between the German and Japanese organizations. This difference is shown in Figure 2-6. As can easily be seen from Figure 2-6, the German subsidiaries are considerably more bureaucratic. It could be argued that this finding, too, is a reflection of increased size which leads to perceived loss of control, as has been suggested by Katz and Kahn,[50] Blau and Scott,[51] and Blau and Schoenherr.[52] Although this factor may indeed be relevant, other researchers such as Franko,[53] Yoshino,[54] Hayashi,[55] and Clark,[56] studying corporations from a comparative perspective, have found that, regardless of size, U.S. multinationals are the most bureaucratized, Japanese the least, and Europeans inbetween. In other words, Japanese and European MNCs tend to control their subsidiaries through personnel.

If the Japanese corporations are indeed relying more on the "personal mode" for control purposes, this strategy should be reflected in the personnel policies of the subsidiary; that is, there should be a significantly greater proportion of expatriates, a greater frequency of visits between headquarters and the subsidiary, and a transfer of managers from subsidiary to subsidiary.[57]

Figure 2-7 shows the number of expatriates and third-country nationals (TCNs) in the German and Japanese subsidiaries studied. As can be seen, both German and Japanese organizations used expatriates for their upper-level management positions. Japanese subsidiaries, however, have had larger numbers of expatriates in middle and lower management and in technical positions. The Japanese executives interviewed explained such staffing patterns on the basis of communication needs, that is, the need to communicate quickly and effectively with their counterparts at headquarters. Our observation suggests that this reason is only a partial explanation and that such staffing patterns reflect a desire to monitor, control, and take corrective action with minimum delay.

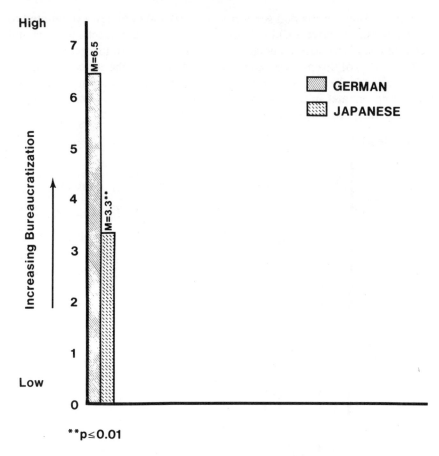

Figure 2-6. Comparison of bureaucratic control indices for German and Japanese subsidiaries.

Our studies also indicated that visits by Japanese headquarter personnel to subsidiaries as well as subsidiary personnel to headquarters were substantially greater than by personnel in German corporations. As Jaeger[58] points out, the personal mode requires that members become familiar with the cultural values and behavior patterns of the organization. Frequent visits are a key element of this enculturation or socialization process. Rohlen[59] has argued that conscious efforts are made by Japanese organizations to "capture" their employees through intensive and conscious use of picnics, parties, or other rituals. Japanese subsidiaries in the United States were no exception. Personnel from American companies acquired by Japanese MNCs were given numerous opportunities to visit Japan, ostensibly to familiarize themselves with the facilities available at headquarters. The actual activities involved during such visits—welcome parties, dinners with

Japanese counterparts and superiors, and cultural evenings – all pointed to a subtle but effective enculturation process. Annual budget meetings and planning sessions also included some kind of enculturation activities. The effectiveness of this process can be seen by comparing the effective turnover rates in the United States, which are in excess of 30 percent annually, with the turnover rates in the Japanese subsidiaries, which were less than 5 percent annually, in practically all of the subsidiaries studied.

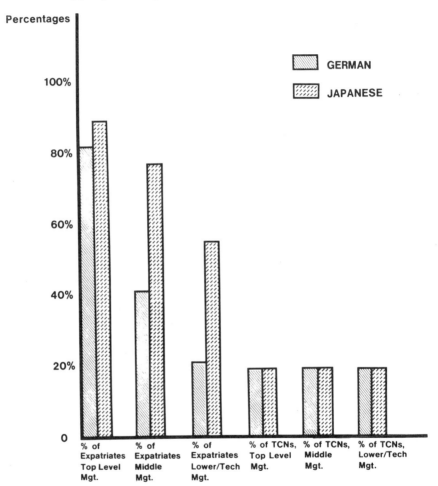

Figure 2-7. Comparison of staffing patterns for German and Japanese subsidiaries.

It is necessary to point out here, however, that Japanese subsidiaries operating in the developing countries have considerable problems with their employees.[60] Most of the problems appear to result from a lack of cultural sensitivity on the part of the Japanese expatriate management. Such insensitivity was demonstrated by enforcing the Japanese style of management (e.g., company songs and deemphasis of role status, which was in contrast to many of the social and professional practices in the host countries). These practices were corrected only after a fair amount of strikes, rioting, absenteeism, and turnover was experienced by the Japanese companies in those countries. The Japanese seem to have benefited a great deal from these experiences as they seem to handle their employees in a more sensitive manner in the United States.

Interactions during visits between German subsidiary personnel and headquarters were generally confined to the problems or issues at hand. The duration and frequency of the visits were relatively shorter, too. Turnover rates were in between those of the American and Japanese firms. These findings also suggest the use of the bureaucratic mode of control over the personal mode by the German multinationals.

Although we did not specifically gather data on the transfers of subsidiary managers, we did learn that such transfers were prevalent. Most Japanese subsidiary executives, however, stayed in a particular subsidiary long enough to become sufficiently well established. Generally, they then moved to other subsidiaries that were being set up. It could be argued that such movement reflected more a need for experienced executives in a period of explosive growth in overseas investment by Japanese MNCs and less a reflection of deliberate efforts at enculturation. As a matter of fact, Japanese executives interviewed felt that international exposure to the largest possible number of Japanese personnel was invaluable. Postings in subsidiaries were viewed as a management development tool. We feel that no matter what motivations were involved the effective outcome was one of enculturation and socialization of the type suggested by Edstrom and Galbraith for the European multinationals.[61]

INTEGRATING MECHANISMS AND INFORMATION FLOWS

The use of subsidiary inputs into the management of the total multinational system is a measure of the respectability accorded to the subsidiary. This involvement can be either ad hoc or formalized through such integrating mechanisms as standing committees, teams, and so on. Our inquiry indicated that there were very few formalized integrating mechanisms for either Japanese or German subsidiaries. Furthermore, as is evident from Figure 2-8, there was surprisingly little strategic information exchange between subsidiaries and headquarters for both the German and the Japanese subsidiaries. This finding could be interpreted as providing the subsidiaries with a great deal of autonomy; but it does not seem to be a very

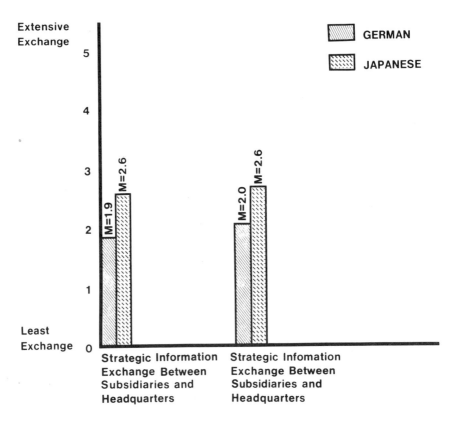

Figure 2-8. Comparison of strategic information exchange between headquarters and subsidiaries of German and Japanese subsidiaries.

valid interpretation for the German subsidiaries in the light of our previous discussions about the influences of the subsidiary in decisionmaking.

For the smaller-sized Japanese subsidiaries, the need for such formal integration mechanisms may have been minimized. Japanese subsidiaries also have another characteristic that may reduce the need for such mechanisms. Most Japanese manufacturing subsidiaries—especially those that were not acquired—are affiliated with a legally separate marketing subsidiary that serves to link the former unit with the respective division at headquarters. In such situations, the president of the marketing subsidiary also usually holds a senior executive position in the international division at corporate headquarters. This, however, does not imply that the manufacturing subsidiary personnel were not in contact with headquarters. On the contrary, there was almost daily contact through telephone calls and telex messages, and in many instances, important decisions were made verbally. Such communications probably reduced the need for formalized integrating mechanisms for operational decisions in the Japanese subsidiaries. The long-range plan and strategies are generally discussed at the annual meeting in Japan.

German subsidiaries seemed to use similar integrating devices. The subsidiary executives generally were on the management boards at headquarters. They also employed annual review meetings to discuss and review long-range plans and strategies.

The Coupling Issue

It has been argued that loosely coupled systems are better than tightly coupled ones in terms of reacting to the environment when the environment is uncertain and turbulent. In the preceeding section, we showed that Japanese subsidiaries had a relatively greater degree of delegation (Figures 2-3 and 2-4) and a lower degree of bureaucratic control (Figure 2-6) as compared to German subsidiaries. This should, presumably, give the former a greater degree of flexibility in reacting to the environment. It could be argued that the smaller size of the Japanese subsidiaries may be responsible for the higher degree of their autonomy, and that the Japanese probably adopted policies deliberately designed to keep the size of their operations small in order to provide greater delegation of authority to the subsidiaries.

Clark[62] reports that the preferred Japanese growth strategy was to spawn off subsidiaries instead of creating new divisions. This policy was encouraged, and, in fact, until 1977, Japanese corporations did not have to report consolidated statements, for the sales and profits of the subsidiaries could be treated separately from that of the parent company. The subsidiary was encouraged to grow independent of the parent, thus providing it with a high degree of flexibility in reaction to environmental stimuli. Japanese firms have continued this practice with their subsidiaries abroad as a matter of policy. Mitsui's president expresses such thinking:

> It is true that by forming a group, business procedures become easier, but this ideology may lead to an easy-going attitude and result in deterioration of working spirit. To strengthen the unity of the group is very important (i.e., move toward tighter coupling) but it is more important for the individual enterprise to establish a strong business structure by its own power.[63]

He further asserts that "the conglomerate of the U.S. is not an acceptable form of grouping as it is contrary to the company's philosophy of not expanding a group by absorbing smaller firms."[64] He endorses progress that is achieved by the independent efforts of member firms. NTN labels this loose-coupling approach as the *Group Management System*. Their policy manual, relating to the establishment of overseas manufacturing facilities, states explicitly:

Based on our small-sized group-management system, we will build a new plant of the same size at different places instead of expanding the existent plant. It means that we shall have two or three plants in the country.[65]

Such deliberate efforts provide the subsidiary operation with a relatively autonomous status. This strategy also avoids problems associated with large size. For example, it has been shown that management has to cope with numerous critical problems once the number of employees exceeds 500.[66] The management at Japanese headquarters appears to be convinced that it is advisable to sacrifice a certain degree of efficiency in order to be effective in handling the interdependencies created by the MNC system. In addition, with larger numbers of small subsidiaries, in contrast to one large, technically efficient plant, patronage can be distributed over a wider area which leads to potential increases in leverage. Further implications of this theory are discussed in the following sections and in Chapter 3.

LEVERAGE

The ability of an organization to achieve its objectives depends greatly on its leverage (bargaining power). The subsidiary leverage is a function of:

1. The specific resources possessed by the organization such as technology, capital, management know-how, and so on.
2. The availability of these resources or attributes from other segments of the organization.
3. The need for the resources.

Furthermore, the leverage possessed by a subsidiary will be reduced if the subsidiary under consideration is a key unit in the total system of the MNC.

It is not surprising to learn that in the United States the bargaining power of subsidiaries of foreign multinational corporations is very limited. This situation is primarily because of the strength of the economy, which generates a wide variety of products and services to meet almost any conceivable need. As a result, the need for any specific product or service is minimal. As a consequence, the leverage possessed by either Japanese or German subsidiaries is extremely low. The leverage of German firms, however, is marginally higher than that of the Japanese subsidiaries, which reflects the use of more sophisticated technoloy by the German firms in our sample.

Even though the leverage of the subsidiaries is very low, there are situations in which the subsidiaries could increase their leverage enormously. These situations arise from the fact that economic developments and benefits are not distributed equally across the United States. Regional or local authorities, such as chambers of commerce, city governments, and so on, are willing to make attractive concessions to multinationals in order to encourage plant locations in their communities. Next we will cite two cases, one German and the other Japanese, that illustrate the manner in which subsidiaries obtained and exploited their leverages — or bargaining positions.

The VW Case

Blinded by the success of the VW Beetle in the United States, Volkswagen had been unaware of the inroads made by the Japanese manufacturers, Toyota and Nissan (Datsun), into their market segment. In 1975, following the Arab oil embargo and its ripple effect, Toyota surpassed VW as the leading importer. Simultaneously, VW was having financial, labor, and political troubles at home. Moreover, the de facto devaluation of the U.S. dollar vis-à-vis the German mark was making the newer cars — the Rabbits — less price competitive. As a consequence, VW was looking for sites in the United States and made this fact widely known. The benefits sought to be derived from this plant were:

1. To reduce the impact of currency fluctuations.
2. To provide management with greater flexibility to react to U.S. market conditions.
3. To reduce shipping costs.
4. To provide some relief to the German employees who were fearful of losing their jobs by using engines and transmissions manufactured in Germany.

All in all, it was apparent that the U.S. subsidiary was seen as being of critical importance to VW's future.

Interestingly, however, the decision to build a plant in the United States coincided with a politically sensitive recession and high unemployment in the United States. As a result, local government officials were looking for new plants to bring jobs and tax revenues.[67] For those reasons, a number of state governments competed with each other in providing the best possible incentives to VW for locating the plant in their respective states. The choice narrowed down to two states: Pennsylvania and Ohio. Ultimately, Pennsylvania offered an incentive package that VW could not turn down. This package consisted of:

1. A $40 million loan at 1.8 percent interest with no principal payments for twenty years.
2. A $6 million loan from the state's school pension fund at 8 percent interest.

3. Two bond issues totaling $25 million to pay for enlarging railroad and highway facilities.

By comparison, VW's financial investment was $250 million. Targeted employment was 5000. The United Auto Worker's Union also lobbied extensively in favor of VW's decision to build a plant in the United States.

The leverage possessed by VW in the above example is obvious in terms of the concessions that it was able to secure from the state of Pennsylvania. In addition, they were also able to obtain concessions from the United Auto Workers in terms of the wages and benefits paid to the employees at the plant. When a section of the workers went on a wildcat strike with the slogan "No money — no bunny," Mr. Schmucker, Chairman of VW, threatened to close down U.S. operations. He could afford to make this threat for the following reasons:

1. Sales of VWs were booming in West Germany.
2. Sales of VWs were also booming in the United States, following the oil crisis.
3. Rabbits commanded a premium price.
4. The relative appreciation of the mark was no longer an important consideration.

VW's vulnerability was far lower than it was at the time of its initial decision to invest. Douglas Fraser, President of the United Auto Workers, apparently recognized these facts and exerted considerable pressure to contain the strike.[68] It is clear that a significant amount of leverage was derived from the employment generated rather than the technology of operations, capital investment, or management know-how.

The Ataka Steel Company Case

This case of a Japanese company setting up a steel mill at Auburn, New York, is considerably similar to the V.W. case described above. In the 1960s, Auburn was a declining industrial town when Mayor Paul Lottimore persuaded Kyoei Steel and Ataka Company (a large Japanese trading firm) to locate a steel mill there. As the area was designated by the state of New York as a high unemployment area, the investors qualified for a ten-year holiday from paying state income taxes. In addition, the Auburn Industrial Development Authority sold $20.5 million in bonds, thus limiting the Japanese investment to only $11.5 million. In addition, the Auburn Industrial Development Authority owns the plant and rented it to Auburn Steel for twenty years, after which ownership will be transferred to the company.[69] Employment potential and, to a limited extent, economic development potential were the main sources of leverage for the Japanese company.

Both cases indicate that by and large the German and Japanese subsidiaries in the United States, and for that matter any other foreign subsidiaries, lack leverage from a national perspective; however, they are able to exercise a certain amount of leverage at local or regional levels. This type of leverage is not significantly different from that exercised by large domestic firms operating in the same or similar regions. Similar investments in the developing countries, on the other hand, would have commanded a tremendously greater amount of leverage at the national level, thus greatly increasing the range of strategies and stances that could be utilized by the multinationals.

The cases discussed above are really not exceptions. As a matter of fact, with economic growth stagnating in the United States, more and more state governments are setting up offices abroad to attract foreign investment and are also willing to offer substantial incentives. If the current economic trends persist in the foreseeable future, we are likely to see an increase in the leverage of foreign subsidiaries operating in the United States. In addition to VW and Honda, BASF, Marubeni, Schott Optical, and Y.K.K. are some of the other German and Japanese subsidiaries that have taken full advantage of incentives offered at local and regional levels.

SUMMARY

In this chapter, we examined similarities and differences in management orientation, headquarter–subsidiary relationships, and leverage possessed by the subsidiaries of German and Japanese multinational companies operating in the United States. Our findings indicate that the Japanese management style is considerably more employee and community oriented than the German orientation. The underlying reasons for these differences in management orientation were also discussed in some detail. Headquarter–subsidiary relationships were found to be relatively more bureaucratized in the German firms as compared to the Japanese subsidiaries, which relied more on personal control. In other words, the Japanese subsidiaries portrayed the following characteristics:

Consensual decisionmaking.
Implicit, informal control with some explicit formalized measures.

The more sophisticated technology and the larger size of German subsidiaries gave rise to a higher level of centralization in decisionmaking. The leverage possessed by the subsidiaries was very weak, from a national perspective, but at the regional and local levels it was strong, especially for the German subsidiaries. The inherent strength of the American economy and the number of alternatives or substitutes available for the specific resources in the U.S. economy were responsible for the weak bargaining positions afforded to the foreign multinationals. This picture may change, however, if the employment situation and general economic conditions in the United States were to deteriorate further.

In the following chapter we will discuss the effects of management orientation, headquarter-subsidiary relationships, and leverage on the strategies and stances undertaken by the German and Japanese subsidiaries studied. The effects of these variables on organizational performance are also discussed.

NOTES

1. For a general discussion of the Japanese management style, see M.Y. Yoshino, *Japan's Managerial System: Tradition and Challenge* (Cambridge, Mass.: MIT Press, 1968); and Ronald Dore, *British Factory-Japanese Factory* (Berkeley: University of California Press, 1973).
2. YKK, *The World of YKK, 1977-78*, p. 1.
3. R. Winslury, "The Managers of Japan," in *Modern Japanese Management* (London: British Institute of Management, 1970), p. 20.
4. Yoshino, *Japan's Managerial System*, ch. 1.
5. S. Terkel, *Working* (New York: Pantheon Books, 1972).
6. Ibid.
7. E.E. Lawler III, *Motivation in Work Organizations* (Monterey, Calif.: Brooks/Cole Publishing Company, 1973).
8. R. Johnson and W. Ouchi, "Made in America: Under Japanese Management," *Harvard Business Review*, Vol. 52, No. 1 (January-February 1974): 61-69.
9. L. Minard, "Good Morning Mr. Kitano," *Forbes,* Vol. 22, No. 8 (August 1978): 104-114.
10. L. Weymouth, "Meet Mr. Sony: How Japanese Outsmart Us," *The Atlantic*, Vol. 244, No. 5 (November 1979): 42.
11. John S. McClenahen, "Cultural Hybrids: Japanese Plants in the U.S.," *Industry Week*, Vol. 202 (February 19, 1979): 73-75.
12. A.R. Negandhi and B.R. Baligan, *Quest for Survival and Growth: A Comparative Study of American, European, and Japanese Multinationals* (New York: Praeger Publishers, and Königstein, West Germany: Athenäum, 1979).
13. R. Clark, *The Japanese Company* (New Haven: Yale University Press, 1979).
14. Quoted in McClenahen, "Cultural Hybrids," p. 74.
15. Weymouth, "Meet Mr. Sony."
16. A Pettigrew, "Information Control as a Power Resource," *Sociology: The Journal of the British Sociological Association*, Vol. 6, No. 2 (May 1972): 97-204.
17. L.G. Franko, *The European Multinationals* (Stamford, Conn.: Greylock Publishers, 1976).
18. J. Child and A. Kieser, "Organizational and Managerial Roles in British and Western German Companies — An Examination of the Cultural Free Thesis," paper presented at the Third International Conference of Cross Cultural Psychologies, Tillurg, West Germany, 1976.
19. Negandhi and Baliga, op. cit.
20. M. Ways, *The Future of Business: Global Issues in the 80s and 90s* (New York: Pergamon Press, 1979).
21. This is Mitsui, (Tokyo: Comercio Japones, Ltd., 1974).

22. *The 100 Year History of Mitsui & Co., Ltd. 1876–1976* (Tokyo: Mitsui & Co., Ltd., 1977), pp. 252–279.
23. Yoshino, *Japan's Managerial System.*
24. T.P. Rohlen, *For Harmony and Strength: Japanese White Collar Organization in Anthropological Perspective* (Berkeley: University of California Press, 1974).
25. M. Yoshino, "Emerging Japanese Multinational Enterprises," in E.F. Vogel (ed), *Modern Japanese Organization and Decision-Making* (Berkeley: University of California Press, 1973).
26. Clark, *The Japanese Company*, pp. 130–131.
27. R.T. Pascale, "Communication and Decision Making Across Cultures: Japanese and American Comparisons," *Administrative Science Quarterly*, Vol. 23, No. 1, (March 1978): pp. 99–109.
28. Johnson and Ouchi, "Made in America".
29. M. Weber, *The Theory of Social and Economic Organizations*, translated by T. Parsons (New York: The Free Press, 1947).
30. M. Duerr and J.M. Roach, *Organization and Control of International Operations (New York: The Conference Board, 1973).*
31. Vogel, *Modern Japanese Organization.*
32. Franko, *The European Multinationals.*
33. McClenahen, "Cultural Hybrids."
34. Ibid.
35. "Japan Pressured for Stateside Auto Plant," *Business Week*, November 8, 1976, p. 40.
36. "Sony's U.S. Operations Go in for Repair," *Business Week*, March 13, 1978, pp. 31–32.
37. Ibid.
38. McClenahen, "Cultural Hybrids."
39. Ibid.
40. H.I. Ansoff, *Business Strategy* (London: Penguin, 1969).
41. P.R. Lawrence and J.W. Lorsch, *Organization and Environment* (Homewood, Ill.: Richard D. Irwin, 1967).
42. J. Child, "Organization Structure and Strategies of Control: A Replication of the Aston Study," *Administrative Science Quarterly*, Vol. 17, No. 2 (June 1972): 163–177.
43. W.G. Ouchi, "The Relationship Between Organizational Structure and Organizational Control," *Administrative Science Quarterly*, Vol. 22, No. 7 (1977): 97.
44. A. Edstrom and J.R. Galbraith, "Transfer of Managers as a Coordination and Control Strategy in Multinational Corporations," *Administrative Science Quarterly*, Vol. 22, No. 2 (1977): 248–263.
45. J.K. Ryans, Jr., and J.H. Donnelly, "Standardized Global Marketing, A Call As Yet Unanswered," *Journal of Marketing*, Vol. 33, No. 2 (April 1969): 57–60.
46. L.G. Franko, *European Business Strategies in the United States* (Geneva: Business International, 1971), 29–42.
47. W.K. Brandt and J.M. Hulbert, "HA Guidance in Market Strategy in the Multinational Subsidiary," *Columbia Journal of World Business*, Vol. 12, No. 4 (Winter 1977): 7–14. Also see J.D. Whitt, "Multinationals in Latin America — An Accent on Control," *Management Accounting,* Vol. 58, No. 8 (February 1977): 49–51.
48. R. Tsurumi, "Japanese Banks in U.S. Expanding Domestic Operations," *Pacific Business Quarterly* (November 4, 1980): 10.
49. Ouchi, "Relationship Between Structure and Control."
50. D. Katz and R.L. Kahn, *The Social Psychology of Organizations* (New York: John Wiley, 1966).
51. P.M. Blau and W.R. Scott, *Formal Organizations* (San Francisco: Chandler Publishing Company, 1962).
52. P.M. Blau and R.A. Schoenherr, *The Structure of Organizations* (New York: Basic Books, 1971).

53. Franko, *European Business Strategies.*
54. M. Yoshino, *Japan's Multinational Enterprises* (Cambridge, Mass.: Harvard University Press, 1976).
55. K. Hayashi, "Corporate Planning Practices in Japanese Multinationals," *Academy of Management Journal,* Vol. 21, No. 2 (June 1978): 211–226.
56. Clark, *The Japanese Company.*
57. Edstrom and Galbraith, "Transfer of Managers."
58. A. Jaeyer, "An Investigation of Organizational Culture in the Multinational Context," paper presented at the 39th Annual Meeting, Academy of Management, Atlanta, 1979.
59. Rohlen, *For Harmony and Strength.*
60. Negandhi and Baliga, *Quest for Survival,* chs. 2 and 3.
61. Edstrom and Galbraith, "Transfer of Managers."
62. Clark, *The Japanese Company.*
63. *This is Mitsui,* p. 38.
64. Ibid.
65. *NTN Overseas Operations* (Tokyo: NTN HQ, 1972), p. 11.
66. Child, "Organization Structure."
67. "The War for the Rabbits," *Newsweek,* May 3, 1976, p. 66.
68. "Volkswagen Hops the Rabbits to Prosperity," *Fortune,* August 13, 1979, pp. 120–129.
69. "The War for the Rabbits," *Newsweek,* May 3, 1976, p. 66.

Chapter 3

Organizational Strategies of the German and Japanese Subsidiaries in the United States

In Chapter 2, we examined the differences between German and Japanese subsidiaries operating in the United States. Specifically, we discussed the similarities and differences in their management orientation, headquarter–subsidiary relationships with special emphasis on decision-making autonomy for the subsidiary, and the relative levels of leverage they possess. In this chapter we will examine the strategies and practices adopted by the German and Japanese subsidiaries and their impact on organizational performance measured in terms of efficiency and effectiveness. To place our discussion in the proper perspective, we will first examine the underlying reasons for direct foreign investment in the United States and then discuss the investment criteria adopted by the German and Japanese subsidiaries studied.

DIRECT INVESTMENT IN THE UNITED STATES

As noted in Chapter 1, foreign direct private investment in U.S. manufacturing has grown rapidly over the last two decades. During the 1970s, it increased more than 3½ times the 1960 level, reaching $70 billion at the end of 1978. About 60 percent of the investment involved construction of new plants or expansion of existing ones, while 40 percent was devoted to acquisitions. This investment, however, represents only about half of the U.S. investment abroad, which was $148 billion in 1978.[1] A number of factors have been cited as responsible for this reverse flow of investment:[2]

1. The de facto devaluation of the U.S. dollar against the West German mark and the Japanese yen.
2. The relatively "open-door" policy followed by successive U.S. federal and state governments to attract investment from abroad.
3. A fear of a potential wave of protectionist policies that could hamper exports to the United States. A number of Japanese firms are especially fearful of this threat.
4. Skilled manpower available in the United States.
5. Investor confidence in the relative political stability within a democratic framework.
6. Well-developed capital market that readily provides credit at very favorable interest rates.[a]
7. Technological leadership in many fields with extensive research and development capabilities.
8. Relatively large supplies of important natural resources.
9. Poorer investment climate outside the United States because of political and labor unrest.
10. The ability of the U.S. economy to ride out the unstable situation caused by high energy prices and sluggish international growth as compared to other national economies.
11. The availability of a large domestic market that has been traditionally receptive to new products, methods, and ideas.

Vernon has argued that significant factors in the decision to invest in the United States are:

1. To learn from the U.S. market to *compete abroad with U.S. companies*.
2. To establish a measure of global equilibrium through creating a balance of mutual threats.[3]

To determine the primary criteria for overseas investment and to ascertain the similarities and differences in investment motivation between the German and Japanese subsidiaries, the executives were asked to respond to a set of questions about investment criteria. The findings are shown in Figure 3–1. As can be seen, favorable labor conditions, availability of capital, and favorable investment incentives played a relatively insignificant part in the

---

[a]This was true until early 1980 when the Federal Reserve began tightening credits and money supply to control inflation.

investment decisions for both the German and Japanese subsidiaries. A desire to preempt U.S. competition in the respective home markets of the MNCs and, to a slightly lesser extent, the desire to exploit technological capabilities appear to be the dominating forces behind the investment decisions. While many U.S. companies have found the large U.S. market attractive enough to preclude the need for investing abroad, the German and Japanese companies are compelled to enter into the U.S. markets because of their limited domestic markets. These executives obviously feared that if they did not establish a base in the United States, this large market would be foreclosed to them forever. Japanese executives interviewed felt that this pressure was mainly caused by the series of court cases brought against some of the Japanese companies under the dumping and other unfair trade practice laws prevailing in the United States.

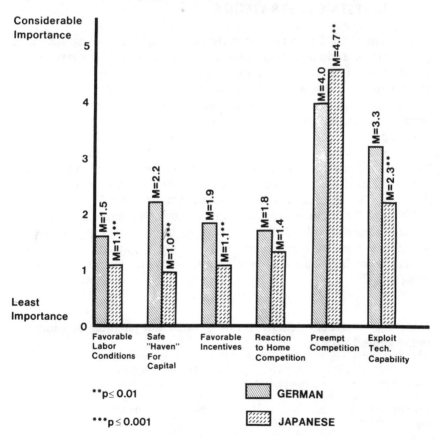

Figure 3-1. Comparison of investment criteria used by German and Japanese subsidiaries.

Japanese companies also seemed to invest in the United States to overcome nontarrif barriers, such as import quotas and the threat of protectionist sentiments. A number of Japanese executives interviewed responded to the affirmative to the question, "Would you prefer to export to the United States in contrast to manufacturing here if you were given the opportunity to do so?" Almost all the products that were currently being manufactured in the United States by Japanese subsidiaries had originally been exported to the United States.[4] Large retail chains, such as Sears, J.C. Penney, and Montgomery Ward assisted the Japanese manufacturing in the United States by providing them with specifications for the U.S. markets and with sizeable orders.

INVESTMENT STRATEGIES

There are basically four different strategies the companies can follow: (1) expansionary; (2) status quo or maintaining of the existing investment; (3) rescue in which the company seeks merger with another organization in order to avert declining sales, profits, or both; (4) disinvestment or harvesting in which an organization is moving toward discontinuing its operation and is trying to obtain the best possible returns during the interim period.

Our interviews with company personnel indicated that the majority of the German subsidiaries (76 percent) and all of the Japanese subsidiaries were expanding in the United States, whereas no one interviewed indicated a desire to either merge or disinvest from the United States.

Although the marketing function was considerably emphasized in the expansion strategies, Table 3-1 shows that a slightly higher proportion of the Japanese companies placed more emphasis on market penetration and diversification in an unrelated field for generating growth than the German subsidiaries.

Table 3-1. Marketing Strategies of German and Japanese Subsidiaries in the United States

Ownership	Market Penetration	Vertical Integration	Related Diversification	Unrelated Diversification
German	4/44.4	1/100	10/62.5	2/28.6
Japanese	5/56.6	0/0	6/37.5	5/71.4
	9/100	1/100	16/100	7/100

Germans, confident about their technological know-how, have preferred to stay in "known waters," whereas the Japanese companies seem to be willing to take on anything that would provide them with the needed experience for manufacturing in industrialized Western countries, for, thus far, their manufacturing experience has been limited to the developing countries. (Approximately 75 percent of the Japanese manufacturing investment is located in the developing countries.)[5] The Japanese subsidiaries that were diversified were generally associated with the trading houses. The extent of unrelated diversification is illustrated in Table 3-2, which shows the manufacturing and nonmanufacturing activities of Mitsui in the United States.

Table 3-2. Mitsui Investments in the United States

Manufacturing Company	Products
Alumax Inc.	Aluminum and processed aluminum products
National Plywood Inc.	Processing and sales of plywood, hardboard, and fiberboard
Oralco Inc.	Aluminum
Weld Loc Systems Inc.	Polypropylene strapping

Nonmanufacturing

Nonmanufacturing investments range from wool products, lumber, real estate, seafood sales, tropical fruit cultivation through textile distribution, fertilizer and grain storage, etc.

Source: Compiled from the company's literature and other news items.

A number of factors influencing diversification have been identified; the significant factors are:

1. Use of financial resources
2. Transferability of new skills
3. Resource abundance and barriers to growth in the home market
4. High growth rate potential in overseas markets
5. Domestic and international competitive positions
6. Horizontal and vertical integration opportunities

The German subsidiaries in the United States emphasized factors 1, 2, and 5, while the Japanese companies considered factor 3 to be more important. If the growth and development of the German chemical giants operating in the United States are examined — Hoechst, Bayer, and BASF — diversification is basically centered around their central technological core. This trend is indicated by their product lines, which comprise dye stuff, agro-chemicals, fibers, pharmaceuticals, plastics, and various intermediate organic and inorganic chemicals. Some exceptions to this trend, however, have started emerging recently. Endowed with cash resources resulting from the appreciation of the German mark vis-à-vis the U.S. dollar, coupled with depressed stock prices, some of the larger German chemical firms have gone on an acquisition binge. Hoechst, for instance, acquired Foster-Grant, a maker of sunglasses. Bayer acquired Miles Labs, producer of Alka-Seltzer and the dietetic breakfast foods line, Morning Star Farms. Apparently, these acquisitions were made to avoid dependency on the chemical lines, which have come under increased cost pressure because of increased petrochemical prices, overcapacities, problems with environmental pollution agencies, and entry into the chemical field by the majority of U.S. rubber and tire manufacturers.

As mentioned earlier, the dumping charges, an increasingly huge surplus in balance of trade and payment positions of Japan vis-à-vis the United States and the other Western industrialized countries, and the growing protectionist sentiments in the United States and elsewhere compelled the Japanese firms to explore the idea of establishing manufacturing subsidiaries in the Western countries. In this regard, their previous experience in the developing countries was not of much help. Japanese success in that part of the world was more a function of political sensitivity and less because of the appropriate marketing and investment strategies used.[6]

Given the strong marketing orientation in the United States, the success of a firm is dependent upon its marketing strategies, that is, augmenting and maintaining market share, effective promotion, and product diversification policies. Thus, as we discussed earlier, both the German and the Japanese firms in the United States emphasized their marketing parameters. In addition, Japanese subsidiaries, besides importing sizeable amounts of machinery and spare parts, also imported considerable amounts of finished and semifinished goods and raw materials from Japan. Such Japanese practices in the developing countries were viewed as an "input control" to protect their interest in joint ventures.[7] In the United States, however, this strategy served to overcome non tariff import barriers and dampened rising anti-Japanese sentiments. In other words, "minimanufacturing" operations were used as a "front" for continuing imports from Japan. For many Japanese manufacturing companies in the United States, the proportion of imported finished and semifinished goods to goods made in the United States was as high as 80 percent.

To sum up, for the Japanese companies the basic motivation to invest in manufacturing activities in the United States was to:

1. Avoid or minimize the effects of tariff and nontariff barriers.
2. Create an "American" identity for the Japanese product.
3. Provide an avenue for the introduction of other goods manufactured by the parent or other affiliates in Japan.
4. Import machine tools, parts, raw materials, and intermediate products from Japan.
5. Provide an opportunity to understand the American marketing environment.

6. Provide opportunities for development of a cadre of personnel to run other international subsidiaries.
7. Provide opportunities to tap into American technology without being accused of "stealing."

German companies, on the other hand, have relied more on "knowledge control." A number of the subsidiaries of German corporations operating in the United States used more sophisticated technologies than those used by comparable U.S. firms. A primary motive of German investors in the United States seems to be a desire to exploit their own superior technologies. A recent study by the Battelle Institute, a private research group, indicated that the European companies in general do not enter American markets to acquire U.S. technology but rather to export superior technology that they have developed.[8]

As pointed out by Vernon,[9] the "exchange of threats" also served as a motivation for German investment in the basic chemical and synthetic fiber industries. Recent ventures into chemicals by the U.S. rubber companies have been perceived as a distinct threat to German companies already in the U.S. chemical industry, and the response has been the construction of new plants to ward off such encroachment. Hoechst, for example, is constructing two major plants at Bayport, Texas, to produce styrene monomer and high-density polyethylene and is planning to invest $40 million annually for the next several years.

BASF, with its present investment of $680 million, was planning additional investments in the range of $100 to $500 million in the next few years. During the years 1973 to 1977, Bayer committed $300 million for U.S. projects, thus doubling its U.S. investment; it is planning another $500-million investment for the period 1977 to 1982, thus further strengthening its economic base.[10]

FINANCING OF EXPANSIONARY STRATEGIES

The financial strategy employed by Bayer A.G. is fairly typical of the method used to finance large capital investments by the German firms, especially in the chemical and pharmaceutical industry. Bayer's U.S. operation is owned by the holding company — Rhinechem Corporation — which is owned in turn by the Curacao-based Bayer International Finance Corporation. The purpose of this strategy is to:

Raise money in U.S. dollars as a hedge against currency fluctuations.
To avoid paying 25 percent surtax on bonds and dividends that are payable by foreign companies, as Curacao is linked to a U.S.-Dutch double taxation agreement under which the transfer of U.S. dividends is subject only to a 5 percent withholding tax.

For borrowing, German subsidiaries generally use the services of American banks because many of the German subsidiaries were originally established when there were serious constraints on foreign banking operations in the United States. With the recent liberalization of laws applying to foreign banks in the United States, some subsidiary executives interviewed revealed that subtle pressures were being applied on them to use services offered by German banks in the United States, for a significant proportion of the voting stock of German multinationals is held by German banks.[11] It would be interesting to observe the future relationship between German subsidiaries and German banks in the United States.

Japanese subsidiaries, on the other hand, generally rely on Japanese banking concerns. In so doing, they help to provide substantial growth for the Japanese banks in the United States. With 14 subsidiaries, 208 branches, 49 branch offices, and 25 agencies representing 50 percent of commercial and industrial loans granted by the foreign banks in 1978, Japanese banks have established a firm hold in the U.S. banking industry.[12] Thus, the close ties that exist in Japan between manufacturing firms and banks are being repeated in the United States for the Japanese subsidiaries and Japanese banks.

Given the sizeable debt to equity ratios that Japanese corporations are used to operating within Japan, only the Japanese banks in the United States are conditioned to and willing to offer financing of this kind to the Japanese manufacturing subsidiaries in the United States. Furthermore, the willingness of Japanese banks to make loans half in dollars and half in yens (to obtain the lower Japanese rates) helps to limit the currency exchange fluctuation exposure[13] as well as to provide support for the partial local manufacture and partial importation strategy of Japanese subsidiaries.

MARKETING BEHAVIOR AND RESPONSES

In the pursuit of expansion how do the German and Japanese companies compete with the established U.S. domestic as well as multinational enterprises, and how do they respond to the public policy issues confronting foreign investors in the United States? To answer these questions, we examined in detail the specific marketing behavior of pricing policies and the positions adopted by the companies in dealing with their competitors and other external environmental groups.

Pricing Policies

Almost all of the Japanese subsidiaries studied had initially concentrated on price manipulation. They generally set lower prices than their competitors in order to create the perception of value. Cutting prices also enabled the companies involved to increase their market penetration, which has been shown to be a key success factor in long-term viability and profitability in the United States.[14] Initially, the Japanese companies could afford to cut prices because of a higher degree of automation and a higher level of productivity both at home and in their overseas subsidiaries. More recently, however, the strategy of reducing prices has created problems because of the relative appreciation of the yen vis-à-vis the dollar. Inherent product attributes, such as reliability and greater gas mileage for cars and quality and ease of servicing technical equipment, are now being stressed. As a result of this relative shift in emphasis, a number of Japanese organizations are establishing technical or market research centers in the United States. Toyota, for example, is spending $4 million to establish a research and technical center in Long Beach, California.[15]

The Japanese companies, manufacturing consumer products in the United States, still continue to be involved in producing extensively for private labels. More recently, however, following Sony's lead, they have taken steps to establish distribution channels as the essential first step in selling directly to the consumer. Companies like Sony and Matsushita have gone one step further by selling some products like videotape recorders to their direct competitors in the T.V. market — Zenith and RCA, respectively. The strategy behind such a move is to let the American companies, with their greater experience in marketing consumer products in the United States, take the major responsibility of educating the consumer and expanding the demand for the product. Interestingly enough, through such co-optation, the Japanese companies have made it difficult, if not impossible, for their former adversaries to accuse them of dumping in the United States. Not surprisingly, they have no plans to manufacture these products in the United States,[16] confirming the notion advanced earlier that it is the fear of protectionist measures that is ultimately responsible for much of the Japanese investment in the United States.

The marketing approaches adopted by the German subsidiaries were typical of those involved in selling sophisticated products or industrial goods. Even in quasi-consumer products, such as photographic films, the German subsidiary studied concentrated in "specialty film and film products," which were more likely to be used by professionals rather than by amateur photo fans. For chemicals and allied products, there was more emphasis on the physical characteristic of the product and less on pricing, and so forth. Price cuts were resorted to only when conditions of supply exceeded demand.

Organizational Response to Public Policy Issues

How do the German and Japanese companies, operating in the United States, respond to charges and public debates on dumping, unfair trade practices, unemployment created by huge imports from Japan, Germany, and elsewhere? Our interviews indicated that by and large both the German and Japanese subsidiaries adopted a businesslike, cool behavior in responding to the above charges and issues. Only in a few instances, was confrontational behavior exhibited, for example, V.W. with respect to the labor strike.

Particularly with respect to the dumping charges against the Japanese companies, the subsidiary personnel interviewed seemed to exhibit an oscillatory attitude. On the one hand, the Japanese organizations have shown a willingness to let the U.S. Judiciary and other regulatory agencies, such as the Treasury Department, and the International Trade Commission, decide the merits of the case. Simultaneously, and often covertly, they have, on the basis of their close relationship with MITI and the Japanese government, indicated a willingness to work toward the establishment of "voluntary quotas" in order to defuse threats of protectionist measures, such as high tariff and nontariff barriers. At the same time, they have been quick in pointing out to the U.S. public the virtue of the great American tradition of free enterprise. They have also sought to co-opt the consumers and consumer organizations by advocating the theme that the import curbs would mean higher prices for the consumer and would generate an inflationary spiral.

To illustrate such behavior by the Japanese companies, let us examine the recent charges of dumping filed by the U.S. steel companies. The Treasury Department has ruled in favor of the American steel companies and proposed a trigger price system. Simultaneously, however, Robert Strauss, then the U.S. trade negotiator, was working feverishly to develop "orderly marketing agreements based on voluntary limits" to defuse congressional pressures in favor of steel import quotas.[17] The response of the Japanese steel subsidiaries in the United States was to call the Treasury ruling "ridiculous" and "arbitrary." At the same time, MITI officially offered an accommodation by stating: "The Japanese want to help 'alleviate' steel import problems in the U.S. . . . and that Japan wants to cooperate with the U.S. Government on the reference price system."[18] Interestingly enough, more than a year after the trigger price system went into effect, Japanese steel imports were at record levels even at the higher prices.[19] During the trade negotiations between Japan and the United States, the Japanese negotiation team stressed the problems of increasing U.S. exports to Japan, thus diffusing the main problem of Japan's huge balance of trade and payment surplus.

Japan T.V. manufacturers, on the other hand, have adopted a strategy of avoiding future dumping charges by acquiring the T.V. manufacturing facilities of U.S. manufacturers who have been forced to cease their operations as a result of their (Japanese) aggressive exports. This policy of acquiring manufacturing facilities has provided them with an opportunity to legitimize their marketing behavior of aggressive pricing and undercutting competitors. No one can accuse them of "dumping" and causing a loss of American jobs. Instead, now they can claim the behavior of a good American corporate citizen: they employ Americans and control inflation by providing the American consumer with quality products at a low cost. And yet the huge imports of components from the parent companies and affiliates outside the United States continue, although they fail to catch the public eye.

Japanese steel companies, because of the need for large capital investments, could not adopt a strategy of acquiring manufacturing facilities in the United States, but they have shown their willingness to rescue ailing U.S. steel companies with limited financial and technical assistance on numerous occasions.

Overall, as stated earlier, both the German and Japanese subsidiaries, partly because of their low leverage in highly competitive markets in the United States, have chosen to adopt low profiles.

COMPARISON OF ORGANIZATIONAL PERFORMANCE

To examine the performance of the German and Japanese subsidiaries and relate them to their management orientations, strategies, policies, and practices, we obtained two sets of data from the companies studied:

Financial and other measurable input or output indices, such as return on investment, labor productivity, and level of equipment utilization. The data for the companies were then compared with those for the respective industry (2-digit SIC classification). On the basis of these comparisons, each firm was classified in one of the following categories: inferior, below average, average, above average, superior. This measure of performance was termed *Efficiency of the Firm*.

Organizational effectiveness was related to the firm's ability to meet the demand of various environmental groups and external agencies. To collect data on this aspect, during our interviews with the executives, we asked them to discuss the nature of their interactions and the problems they faced with the various groups, such as local, state, and federal government agencies, regulatory departments, labor unions, consumer groups, and environmentalists. Supplementary information on the company interactions were also collected from published sources. On the basis of these interviews and published information, each company was classified on the following scale: minimum or no problems to extensive problems.

Table 3-3 reports the overall results on the firms' efficiency and effectiveness measures discussed above. As evident from the table, there were no

Table 3-3. Comparison of Organizational Performance Measures for German and Japanese Subsidiaries

Criterion	German Subsidiaries (N = 17)		Japanese Subsidiaries (N = 16)	
	Mean	Standard Deviation	Mean	Standard Deviation
Efficiency[a]	3.6	0.48	3.6	0.60
Effectiveness[b]	3.7	0.43	3.8	0.30

[a]The efficiency scale was developed by averaging four criteria, the returns on sales, return on investment, labor productivity, and equipment utilization and measuring them on a five-point scale that ranged from inferior to superior.

[b]The effectiveness scale was derived by measuring the firm's interactions and problems faced with the external publics on a five-point scale that ranged from no problems at all to extensive problems.

significant differences between the German and Japanese subsidiaries in either efficiency or effectiveness criteria. Overall, all the firms studied were average performers.

It is interesting to speculate on the causes for this average performance. The answer, we think, lies in the microeconomic theory of free competition,[20] which asserts that in a truly competitive industry the returns for all firms would tend to be more or less the same. All subsidiaries studied were in fact operating in highly competitive industries. In addition, as discussed earlier, the price of the product was considered an important variable, especially for the Japanese companies in designing the marketing strategy. Some of the diversification strategies of German firms, discussed in earlier sections, also seemed to indicate that the competitiveness was likely to continue into the future.

DISCUSSION OF RESULTS

Our results show that the more humanistic management orientation as well as the relatively higher level of decisionmaking autonomy of the Japanese subsidiaries as compared to the German subsidiaries were not very useful in generating higher operational efficiency. Next, we will speculate why these management orientations and organizational practices have failed to make more of a contribution.

Fromm,[21] and Rogers,[22] among others, have characterized American society as a "transactional" society that shuns intimacy in relationships. This transactional nature has been reinforced in the economic sector mainly through a continued emphasis on confrontational management–union relationships.[23] In addition, increasing levels of automation and emphasis on the technological dimension, in the quest for greater productivity, have reduced the employees in an organization to "one-dimensional men."[24] Clark[25] has stressed that the Japanese management–orientation system can function only when employers and employees perceive a sense of mutual obligation to each other. The current positive attitude of American employees toward the Japanese management orientation may be caused not so much by an inherent appreciation of the system, but by a feeling of relief from getting away from the confrontational American industrial system. Thus, such an attitude may indeed be transitory in nature.

These remarks appear to be in conflict with those made by Brown. He has argued that Western social values are progressively becoming more humanistic.[26] Although in recent years American industry has shown a desire to foster more "humanistic" values in the environment, the necessary emotional as well as financial commitment to that end is still lacking. The spirit of independence and a sense of detachment still appear strong in the United States. The relative failure of T groups and organizational development efforts, directed at integrating the individual with the organization,[27] are further proof of the unwillingness of American employers to commit themselves to a more "humanistic" orientation. Furthermore, management, pressed for short-term survival, as a result of intense competitive pressures and demands, also seems unwilling to devote long-term efforts to reinforce humanistic values within the organization; instead, it seeks technological breakthroughs that increase productivity and decrease dependence on human beings. Rohlen[28] has indicated that although the Japanese employees (in Japan) are remarkably company oriented by contemporary Western standards, exposure to modern living is rapidly eroding this commitment. The possibility for sustained humanistic orientation thus appears bleak. The German subsidiaries, which have been operating here for a longer time than the Japanese, have already shown a convergence in their orientation to that of the American management system. Knoepfel,[29] for example, found that although there were differences in the management styles of the European and American managers he studied, these differences were of little consequence in terms of performance. He claimed that ultimately there was only a "good" or "bad" style of management within the context of a firm's operation. Another reason why management orientation may not be a critical factor for success in the American environment may be the result of the extremely competitive nature of the market and the availability of surplus capacity in many of the industries studied. As a result, an increase in productivity that can be traced to a humanistic management orientation cannot overcome inherent marketing and supply or demand problems.

With respect to the higher autonomy of the Japanese subsidiaries not contributing to higher operational efficiency, we suggest that in a competitive market, such as in the United States, a certain amount of standardization of production and marketing processes and, consequently, a higher level of centralized decisionmaking may be inevitable in generating higher operational efficiency. Conversely, if public demands are fewer, the firm's effectiveness, as we have conceptualized it, may converge with operational efficiency. That is, there may not be any significant differences between these two aspects of performance measures.

On the other hand, if market conditions are less powerful and dominating forces, public demands, and governmental interferences are stronger, greater influence of the management orientation, subsidiary autonomy, and the firm's leverage on both the operational efficiency and the organizational effectivesss would be expected.

Such weaker market conditions and stronger public demands are prevalent in the less developed countries. In the next chapter, therefore, we will discuss the results of our study in the six developing countries. As noted in Chapter 1, although the nature of the study and the measures employed were somewhat different from the study undertaken in the United States, they do provide some useful insights for understanding the similarities and differences among American, European, and Japanese multinational practices pursued in the developed versus the developing countries.

NOTES

1. *Wall Street Journal*, November 27, 1978, p. 30.
2. See (a) "Financing Troubles for VW's New Plant," *Business Week*, July 5, 1976, p. 26; (b) "Role of Foreign Investment in the U.S.," *Nation's Business*, March 9, 1977, p. 57; (c) "U.S. Rabbit All Set to Hop," *Time*, April 10, 1978, p. 84.
3. R. Vernon, *Storm Over the Multinationals: The Real Issues*, (Cambridge, Mass.: Harvard University Press, 1977).
4. They seem to have followed the product life cycle theory. See R. Vernon, *Sovereignty at Bay: The Multinational Spread of U.S. Enterprises,* New York: Basic Books, 1971).
5. Y. Tsurumi, *The Japanese Are Coming,* (Cambridge, Mass.: Ballinger Publishing Company, 1976), p. 4.
6. A.R. Negandhi and B.R. Baliga; *Quest for Survival and Growth: A Comparative Study of American, European, and Japanese Multinationals,* (New York: Praeger Publishers, 1979), ch. 3, pp. 42–43; and (Königstein, West Germany: Athenäum, 1979).
7. Ibid.
8. L.G. Franko, *The European Multinationals*, (Stamford, Conn.: Greylock Publishers, 1976).
9. Vernon, *Storm Over the Multinationals.*
10. "Labor's New Push for Protection," *Business Week*, December 26, 1977, p. 31.
11. G.P. Dyas and H.T. Thanheiser, *The Emerging European Enterprise: Strategy and Structure in French and German Industry*, (London: Macmillan, Ltd., 1976).
12. *Forbes*, September 15, 1976, p. 78.
13. P. Feinberg, "Developing A Global Financing Strategy," *Institutional Investor*, Vol. 12, No. 1 (November 1978): 127–130.

14. R.D. Buzzell, B.T. Gale, and R.G.M. Sultan, "Market Share — A Key to Profitability, *Harvard Business Review,* Vol. 53, No. 7 (January–February 1975): 97–106.
15. "The Japanese Connection," *The Executive* (May 1978): 32LA–35LA.
16. "Nippan Electric Company Plans U.S. Output of Some Equipment," *Wall Street Journal,* January 19, 1977, p. 14.
17. "U.S. to Unveil Steel Aid Plan Tomorrow Amid Support of Industry," *Wall Street Journal,* December 5, 1977, p. 5.
18. Ibid.
19. *Business Week,* March 12, 1979, p. 77.
20. J.M. Henderson and R.E. Qunandt, *Microeconomic Theory: A Mathematical Approach* (New York: McGraw-Hill, 1975).
21. E. Fromm, *Escape from Freedom* (New York: Holt, Rinehart and Winston, 1963); and E. Fromm, *Sane Society* (New York: Fawcett, 1977).
22. C. Rogers, *On Becoming A Person* (Boston: Houghton Miffin, 1961).
23. N.W. Chamberlain and J.W. Kuhn, *Collective Bargaining* (New York: McGraw-Hill, 1965).
24. H. Marcuse, *One Dimensional Man* (Boston: Beacon Press, 1964).
25. R. Clark, *The Japanese Company* (New Haven: Yale University Press, 1979).
26. C.C. Brown, "A Corporate Dilemma: Materialism vs. Humanism," in M. Ways (ed.), *The Future of Business* (New York: Pergamon Press, 1979), pp. 1–18.
27. C. Argyris, *Integrating the Individual and the Organization* (New York: John Wiley, 1964); and C. Argyris, *Management and Organizational Development: The Paths from XA to YB* (New York: McGraw-Hill, 1971).
28. T.P. Rohlen, *For Harmony and Strength: Japanese White Collar Organization in Anthropological Perspective* (Berkeley: University of California Press, 1974).
29. R.W. Knoepfel, "American and European Enterpreneurs and Managers," *Managerial Planning,* Vol. 23, No. 3 (November–December 1974): 1–14.

Chapter 4

Management Orientations of American, European, and Japanese Multinationals in the Developing Countries

In the last two chapters, we examined the management orientations of the German and Japanese subisidiaries operating in the United States. Our inquiry into their investment strategies, diversification policies, marketing strategies, personnel policies, decisionmaking aspects, particularly the relative influence of headquarters and subsidiaries in major policy decisions, the exercise of power and leverage, and the nature of tactics used in dealing with the host country's (U.S.) regulatory agencies and other publics revealed no major differences between these two types of subsidiaries.

To be sure, we did observe minor differences between these two types of subsidiaries, especially in their formalized control procedures, management of the personnel function, and their desires and abilities to rationalize production and marketing processes to achieve economies of scale. In these respects, German subsidiaries were more formalized, both in their decision-making and control processes. They also paid more attention to rationalizing production processes with global level considerations, whereas Japanese subsidiaries operated with relatively autonomous structures and decentralized control systems. In other words, for Japanese subsidiaries, the host

The material in this chapter is drawn from Anant R. Negandhi and B.R. Baliga, *Quest for Survival and Growth: A Comparative Study of American, European, and Japanese Multinationals* (New York: Praeger, and Königstein, West Germany: Athenäum, 1979), pp. 13-63.

country, that is, the U.S. market, was a prime consideration. Japanese welfare-oriented personnel policies (e.g., more extensive employee benefits in terms of job security) seem to have penetrated into their subsidiary operations. Nevertheless, the overall differences between these two types of subsidiaries were not significant enough to affect their relative efficiencies and effectiveness (see Chapter 3).

During the 1960s and 1970s, research in cross-cultural as well as cross-national studies has uncovered significant differences in management styles, orientations, and practices by American, European, and Japanese enterprises, as well as enterprises from developing countries.[1]

U.S. managerial practices and orientations, for example, have been characterized as aggressive, egalitarian, and conscious of human relations. In contrast, European management practices have been described as authoritarian, passive, and paternalistic.[2] Finally, Japanese management has been characterized as paternalistic, culture-bound, and secretive.[3]

Our findings, thus, raise some interesting questions:

1. Is convergence occurring in management practices worldwide? and/or
2. Does convergence in socioeconomic aspirations around the world have an overwhelming impact on management of industrial enterprises? and/or
3. Is the United States a unique phenomenon as a marketplace, in which all enterprises have to fall in line and act similarly in order to survive and grow?

The growing literature on management of multinational corporations provides some evidence for the convergence thesis. For example, studies published under the Harvard Multinational Enterprise Project indicate that as the firm gains experience in international business and grows in size and diversity in its product lines, spreads geographically, and relies on innovation, research, and development activities, it will be compelled to rationalize production and marketing processes to reduce costs and to coordinate its global operations.[4]

Vernon, writing in 1971 about the changing strategies and structures of European multinationals, observed that the European firms "gamble of leaping to a global logistical structure that would match U.S.-controlled enterprise. . . was fully successful.[5]

In his study of Japan-based multinational corporations, Yoshino found that "to arrest the tide of rapidly eroding competitive advantages, Japanese enterprises began to adopt new strategies — strategies that had become quite familiar in U.S.-based multinational enterprises in mature oligopolies. These strategies included: upgrading and broadening product lines; emphasizing product differentiation through marketing means and achieving vertical integration."[6]

Yoshino goes on to say that "his study has also shown that as the Japanese manufacturing enterprises began to pursue strategies similar to those of the U.S.-based multinational enterprises, they too began to manifest definite preference for control."[7]

Lastly, Franko, in his study of Continental European multinational corporations, found that:

> Before World War II . . . only one Continental enterprise managed relations with foreign subsidiaries through a supernational structure (rationalized formal control), even though 14 enterprises manufactured in more than seven countries by 1938. By 1968, the year when tariffs reached zero within the EEC, 12 enterprises had moved to structures with supernational center of responsibility; by 1971 the number was 39 (out of total 60).[8]

To put it simply, the technological and market imperatives are pushing all types of multinationals to pursue global level strategies and structures.[9] Our own findings, as reported in Chapters 2 and 3, for the German and Japanese subsidiaries operating in the United States are consistent with the earlier results of studies undertaken by the Harvard group and others.[10]

WHY DO U.S. MULTINATIONALS HAVE MORE PROBLEMS IN THE DEVELOPING COUNTRIES?

If the managerial strategies and policies of the multinational corporations from different countries or areas (e.g., United States, Europe, Japan) are converging because of the technological and market factor, then one of the perplexing questions that still remains unanswered is: Why do U.S. multinationals seem to have more problems with the developing countries? In other words, what factors, in terms of organizational attributes as well as practices, could explain the seemingly higher levels of conflicts for U.S. multinationals with the developing countries?

To probe into this important question, we undertook a systematic study of American, European, and Japanese multinational corporations in six developing countries: Brazil, India, Malaysia, Peru, Singapore, and Thailand. These six countries were chosen to provide enough diversity in economic and political structures, levels of economic and industrial developments, and varied experience with foreign private investments. In the remainder of this chapter, we will summarize the major findings of this study. Detailed results are reported elsewhere.[11]

ATTRIBUTES AND CONFLICTS OF MULTINATIONALS WITH THE HOST COUNTRIES

A number of assertions have been made by academicians and businessmen alike, pointing out some of the important causes of conflict between the MNCs and the host governments. It has been argued, for example, that the foreign private investor, besides being an "outside intruder," upsets the status quo in the host country for being:

1. Larger in size and capital resources.[12]
2. More aggressive in its marketing strategies, and thereby establishing porportionately higher market shares than the comparable local firms.[13]
3. More sophisticated in its management and technological systems.[14]
4. More efficient.[15]
5. More diversified, and hence more visible in the public eyes.[16]

As the Harvard data bank on multinational corporations[17] indicates, American MNCs seem to have more of the above characteristics than their counterparts, the European and Japanese multinationals. That is, American MNCs are not only bigger in size and capital resources, but are also more research and marketing oriented and more diversified. In their global operations, they also seem to pursue more aggressive marketing and management styles.[18]

Although such a link between the internal attributes of the multinationals and their problems with the host and home countries has been articulated by both scholars and businessmen, there has been no systematic attempt to explore such a relationship. The study reported below attempts to shed some light on the nature of the relationship between the attributes of the MNCs and their conflicts with the developing countries.

RESEARCH RESULTS

To provide some perspectives on the nature of the conflicts of the MNCs with the host countries, we will first briefly outline the conflicting issues encountered by the MNCs operating in the six developing countries.

Conflicting Issues

Table 4-1 provides the results of our interviews with the senior executives of 124 MNCs concerning the conflicting issues confronting them in the six developing countries. As Table 4-1 shows, three issues, equity participation, a desire to retain control in the hands of local nationals, and transfer pricing, dominated the scene. The other issue, such as interference of the MNCs with the host country's socioeconomic norms, was not considered to be a major problem.

A similar trend was also observed by the U.S. State Department, in their analysis of conflicts between U.S. business firms and host governments during the period 1960 through 1971. They found that of the 198 cases of

Table 4-1. Issues That Caused Conflicts Between MNCs and the Host Countries (Interview Responses)

Conflicts	Far East			Latin America			Both Areas			Total[a]
Equity participation by locals	13	14	0	0	0	1	13	14	1	28
Management control in the hands of local nationals	15	17	13	2	3	2	17	20	15	52
Control of exchange	2	3	0	0	1	0	2	4	0	6
Control of imports	3	0	1	0	1	0	3	1	1	5
Expansion of exports	3	2	2	1	1	0	4	3	2	9
Transfer pricing (pricing policies)	6	6	2	5	2	0	11	8	2	21
Use of local inputs	0	2	0	0	0	0	0	2	0	2
Interference by host government in corporate affairs	2	2	0	0	1	0	2	3	0	5
Contributions to economic plans of host nations	2	0	0	2	0	0	4	0	0	4
Interference with sociocultural norms	1	0	1	1	1	0	2	1	1	4
Interference by MNCs home governments with host government policies	1	0	0	1	0	0	2	0	0	2
Total	48	46	19	12	10	3	60	56	22	138
		Total			Total			Total		
		113			25			138		

Source: Interview data reproduced from Anant R. Negandhi and B.R. Baliga, *Quest for Survival and Growth* (New York: Praeger, and Königstein, West Germany: Athenäum, 1979), p. 15. Permission of the publishers is gratefully acknowledged.

[a]This total exceeds the total number of conflicts used in the analysis for some of the types of conflicts had more than one cause; that is, a negotiational conflict, for example, could have resulted from demands for both equity reduction and localization of personnel.

conflicts, 128 were concerned with equity participation. They also reported that conflicts over such issues have been increasing since 1969 (see Table 4-2).

These results reflect certain fundamental changes in the problems faced by the international firms. For example, in the early 1950s and 1960s, it was widely accepted that a significant proportion of the problems confronting international firms related to their difficulties in adapting to the differing sociocultural norms of the host societies. During this era, many believed that solving problems of initial sociocultural adaptation would create unlimited opportunities for the expansion of international business around the world.[19]

As Table 4–1 shows, very few of the problems of the MNCs were related to sociocultural adaptation. Four out of a total of 139 conflicts examined could be traced to sociocultural factors. These results indicate that host governments are more prone to defining their problems with foreign investors in economic terms — equity participation, management control, expansion of exports, reduction of imports, use of local inputs, exchange control, and so on.

Table 4–2. Issues That Caused Conflict Between U.S. Investors and the Host Countries (U.S. State Department Study)

	60	61	62	63	64	65	66	67	68	69	70	71	Total
Equity	—	1	1	—	2	2	1	3	—	5	39	74	128
Participation	—	—	—	1	—	—	—	—	—	—	—	6	7
Pricing policy	—	—	—	—	—	—	—	—	—	—	—	3	3
Controls by government	—	1	1	2	12	—	—	—	1	2	6	25	50
Expansion of exports	—	—	—	—	—	—	—	—	—	—	—	—	—
Interference with host economy	—	1	—	—	—	—	—	—	—	—	1	4	6
Interference with sociocultural norms	—	—	—	—	—	—	—	—	—	—	—	2	2
Interference by MNCs home governments with host government policies	—	—	—	—	—	—	—	—	—	—	—	1	1
Conflict with national sovereignty	—	—	—	—	—	—	—	—	—	—	1	—	1
	—	3	2	3	14	2	1	3	1	7	47	115	198

Source: U.S. State Department, "Disputes Involving U.S. Foreign Investment: July 1, 1971 through July 1, 1973" (Washington, D.C.: Bureau of Intelligence & Research RECS-6, February 8, 1974).

To explore the relationship between the internal attributes of the MNCs and the nature and intensity of conflicts they experienced in the host countries, we created the following four analytical categories of conflict:

1. *Value conflict* was related to the basic belief and value system of a given society. The elements involved in such a conflict went far beyond the actual issues that triggered off the conflict. Such conflicts were very intense.

2. *Negotiational conflict* had its locus in the perception by the host government, the MNC, or both, that some basic terms of contract previously agreed upon, implicitly, or explicitly, had been violated by the opposite party. This type of conflict, in our analytical terms, was conceived as *company-specific*, and took place on a one-to-one basis.

3. *Policy conflict* had its locus in the basic disagreement among the parties over certain policy issues. In contrast to the negotiational conflict, the policy conflict was conceived as *industry-specific*. In other words, a large majority of firms in a given industry were affected by a policy conflict, for example, price and production controls on pharmaceutical products.
4. *Operational conflict* was generally encountered by the MNCs with task or environmental groups (e.g., consumers, suppliers, labor unions, employers) with which the firm dealt in its day-to-day operations.

The first three levels of these conflicts were conceived of in our research as *interface* or *interorganizational conflicts*, while the fourth level of conflict, operational conflict, was regarded as *intraorganizational conflict*.

Our interviews with the 124 MNCs yielded 102 cases of conflict. Interestingly enough, of these cases, only two could be classified as "value" conflicts. As these two cases of value conflict would only accentuate the observed differences, it was decided to omit them for purposes of statistical analysis.

Ownership and Conflict

Table 4-3 provides an association between the controlling ownership of the MNC and the level of MNC–environment unit conflict.[a] As is evident from the table, U.S. MNCs have had more interface conflicts, while Japanese MNCs have had more operational conflicts. It is interesting, however to

Table 4-3. Conflict versus Controlling Ownership of an MNC

	Ownership		
Nature of Conflict	U.S. (N/%)	European (N/%)	Japanese (N/%)
Negotiational	17/39.5	13/38.2	5/21.7
Policy	16/37.2	15/44.2	4/17.4
Operational	10/23.3	6/17.6	14/60.9
	43/100	34/100	23/100
N = 100			

Source: Anant R. Negandhi and B.R. Baliga, *Quest for Survival and Growth* (New York: Praeger, and Königstein, West Germany: Athenäum, 1979), p. 119. Permission of the publishers is gratefully acknowledged.

[a]For brevity, we henceforth refer to MNC–host government conflict and conflicts with various publics in the host country as MNC–environment unit conflicts.

note that there are no significant differences between the American and European corporations. In fact, like U.S. MNCs, the majority of European MNCs also faced negotiational and policy conflicts, whereas merely a fraction of them were plagued with operational problems. In specific terms, the types of interface problems experienced by the U.S. and European MNCs centered around the requirements of the host governments for dilution of equity and management control, reduction or elimination of royalty payments for technology and knowhow, transfer pricing policies, and so on. The operational problems faced by Japanese MNCs were low morale and employee productivity, high turnover and absenteeism, and interpersonal conflicts between Japanese expatriate managers and local personnel.

Although the American and European MNCs faced similar problems overseas, they differed in their modes of resolving their conflicts in the host countries.

Equity Holding and Conflict

Both to monitor the activities of the multinationals and also to harness them for achieving their own national socioeconomic plans, many developing countries have increased their demands for local equity participation and staffing of local nationals at higher managerial positions. Following the examples set by India and Mexico, such demands by the developing countries have now become a rule rather than an exception. Most nations now demand majority equity participation, either by local entrepreneurs, the government itself, or both, in the foreign ventures operating in their countries. The recently enacted Foreign Investment Regulation Act by the Indian Government,[20] the regulations enacted by the Andean Pact countries,[21] and the Malaysian regulation, which demands 40-30-30 ratios in foreign enterprises,[22] exhibit striking similarities in the aspirations and demands of these nations. Such similarities are not accidental. In other words, these regulations represent a growing awareness among the developing countries that their lot is identical, and that like problems require like solutions.

The multinational enterprises, on the other hand, prefer and generally insist upon 100-percent ownership and management control of their subsidiary operations; at the very least, they prefer to retain majority equity and managerial control. Given such differences in expectations on both sides, a certain amount of tension and conflict between the MNCs and the host nations related to equity participation and management control would be expected. As seen in a preceding section (Table 4-1), a large majority of conflicts between MNCs and host governments were indeed centered around these two issues.

For our own study, an overwhelming majority of U.S. subsidiaries (75 percent) where wholly owned by the parent companies, while only a fraction of the subsidiaries of the Japanese MNCs were wholly owned by the parent (26 percent). European MNCs, as in most other instances, resembled the American MNCs, two-thirds of them were wholly owned.[b]

Given these differences in the pattern of equity holding in their subsidiaries, it could be argued that the interface problems faced by American and European multinationals may be caused by their ownership patterns. Conversely, it could also be hypothesized that Japanese MNCs have an easier time with their host governments, as they are willing to settle for minority participation. Our findings indicate significant evidence that confirms this hypothesis. Table 4-4 shows that wholly owned companies have approximately one and a half times more negotiational conflicts with the host countries than those of minority-owned corporations. Our results also show that although the minority-owned foreign companies in the developing countries had complied with equity demands, they were now being confronted with new demands by the host governments. They included demands for increased exports and foreign exchange earnings, localization of management control, reduction in prices, and so forth. All this suggests that the MNCs should not be naive enough to believe that complying with the demands of the host government at a particular time will result in enduring peace.

Market Power and Conflict

One of the major concerns of the host nations about MNCs is that the local industries are being displaced by foreign investors. There is also a genuine fear that the MNCs could become monopolistic powers, beyond the control of the national government. Behrman observed that "Although the host country likes improvement of quality, reduction of prices, increases of wages, etc., resulting from foreign investment, it may not like to see its domestic enterprise pushed to the wall."[23]

In other words, a monopolistic or oligopolistic market power of the multinationals, which could result in a virtual "takeover" of local enterprises, is actively resisted, not only by the developing, but also the industrially developed nations. Countries such as Canada, France, West Germany, and the United Kingdom have enacted regulations to discourage such behavior by foreign investors.[24] Even the United States, the champion of the free-enterprise system, has shown concern about the adverse impact of foreign investments on local enterprises.[25].

[b]This is in contrast to Franko's study of European multinationals. He reports that a larger number of Continental enterprises in the developing countries were joint ventures. Thus our own sample of European MNCs, which were mostly wholly owned, might have caused greater similarities between European and American MNCs. See L.G. Franko, *The European Multinationals* (Palo Alto, Calif.: Greylock Publishers, 1976), pp. 120–122.

Table 4-4. Internal Attributes of MNCs (Subsidiaries) and the Nature of Conflict

Company Attributes (N = 100)	Nature of Conflict			Level of Significance
	Negotiational	Policy	Operational	
Equity Holding	%	%	%	
Wholly owned	36	36	28	
Majority owned	38	27	35	
Minority owned	20	60	20	$p < .08$
Market Share				
More than 60%	40	35	25	
26–59%	33	42	25	
Less than 26%	35	27	38	$p < .4704$
Degree of Competitiveness				
Seller's market	70	30	0	
Moderately competitive	46	37	17	
Highly competitive	25	36	39	$p < .05$
Expectational Difference (between MNCs and host governments)				
Large difference	54	28	18	
Moderate difference	27	59	14	
Little or no difference	21	28	51	$p < .003$
Number of Employees				
More than 1000	40	31	29	
999 to 400	40	40	20	
399 to 100	19	50	31	
Less than 100	17	0	83	$p < .0421$
Size of Investment				
$4.9–$3 million	43	31	26	
$2.9–$2 million	33	42	25	
$1.9–$.5 million	20	40	40	
Less than $500,000	60	40	0	$p < .5315$

Source: Author interviews.

Despite such widespread concern over the adverse impact of market domination by the MNCs in the host countries, our study did not indicate a significant relationship between the market share of the MNCs and the nature of conflicts in the host countries. Although a large proportion of the

MNCs studied indicated that their market share was more than 25 percent, their problems were, in no case, different from those faced by companies whose market share was minimal. In other words, it appears that, regardless of market share, they all were equally susceptible to similar issues and problems. Of the six countries we studied, only in Malaysia, and to some extent in Brazil, did the MNC market share have some impact on the type of problems faced with the government. The overall relationship between these two variables was less striking, however. This lack of relationship does not imply that the developing countries are unconcerned about issues of economic domination by the multinationals. As Table 4–4 shows, the market conditions (degree of competitiveness) faced by the MNCs had a significant relationship with the nature of conflict. Overall, firms facing a seller's market or a moderately competitive market encountered a greater number of negotiational and policy conflicts than firms facing highly competitive markets. (Our results reported in Chapters 2 and 3 for the U.S. market are consistent with these results.)

Expectational Differences and Conflict

Psychologists, political scientists, and other social scientists concerned with the study of human behavior have argued for some time that actual or imaginary differences in expectations between two parties involved in an interaction are likely to result in a breakdown of communication, which may generate tension and even conflict between them. Therefore, to examine whether the differences in expectations led to a breakdown in communication, and consequently generated tension and conflict between MNCs and host governments, we collected information on many items relating to the expectations of the MNCs and the host governments toward each other. Governmental policies, newspaper reports, and other information gathered through personal interviews with executives of the MNCs and government officials in these countries provided additional information about their expectations toward each other.[c] Our results indicate a widening gap between the expectations of the MNCs and the host governments.

In more specific terms, many of the developing countries, in order to maximize their returns from foreign private investment, have enacted legislation that requires a majority of local equity in foreign enterprises, a higher proportion of local nationals in top positions, an increase in exports and foreign exchange earnings, and a reduction in imports of raw material and spare parts.

Such demands from the host countries have, to some extent, constrained the MNCs from rationalizing their worldwide productive capacity. In return, the MNCs have made demands on the host countries to provide

[c]For operationalization of this variable and other variables, see Appendix A.

them with efficient infrastructural facilities, reduce bureaucratic controls and interference in corporate affairs, and provide conducive labor legislation and more flexible expansion policies.

Thus, although the host countries have shown a strong concern over the displacement of local firms by foreign investors, and have demanded the development of local resources, utilization of local supplies, an increase in R&D activities, and local ownership (equity) in foreign enterprises, the MNCs seem to have perceived these demands by the host countries as merely empty noises.

These differences in expectations between the MNCs and the host countries are bound to create tensions and conflicts; our results show a strong association between these two variables. As Table 4-4 shows, therefore, MNCs with larger expectational differences are more often involved in negotiational conflicts with the host governments than MNCs with small expectational differences. Our results also indicate that, relatively speaking, a greater number of U.S. MNCs have had larger expectational differences with the host countries than the European and Japanese MNCs.

The Impact of Other Factors

Our results indicated a very minor impact of such MNC attributes as number of years in operation, the level of technology utilized, type of industry, and level of diversification of MNC–host country conflicts. The results are given in Table 4-4.

Thus, the assertion that MNC attributes, such as size of capital investment, sophistication of technology employed, degree of diversification, period of operation, and sales volume, would have a significant relationship with the level of conflict in the host country fared poorly in the empirical findings. Ownership and pattern of equity holding indicated a substantial relationship with the level of conflict. The fact that expectational differences contributed significantly to the variation in the dependent variable of conflict presents some very important implications for both the host governments and the multinational corporations. It was evident from the data gathered in the field through depth interviews that both host government representative and MNC chief executives have had only a very diffuse understanding of what they expected from each other. While most host governments viewed the entry of MNCs as "the panacea for all economic and social ills," MNC decisionmakers viewed their entry primarily in terms of either entry into a potentially large market or in terms of global rationalization of their operations. Any socioeconomic benefits that accrued to the host were viewed as purely incidental to their main goals.

A surprising finding was the significant relationship between the degree of market competitiveness and conflict, which is indicated in Table 4-4. MNCs operating in moderately competitive and sellers' markets were involved in higher levels of conflict as compared to firms operating in highly competitive markets. We can only hazard a guess as to why this is so. It would appear that firms in a seller's market were under pressure primarily from the government because of their potential monopolistic powers, whereas firms in competitive markets were under pressure primarily from constituents in the task environment. Firms in moderately competitive markets appeared to be under pressure from both segments. The majority of U.S. firms operated either in moderately competitive markets or in highly competitive markets, although they accounted for a signficant proportion of interface conflicts, thus indicating the strong association of ownership of MNCs and MNC–host country conflicts.

In conclusion, it may be noted that a significant amount of variation in the dependent variable — 64 percent — remains unexplained. This probably suggests that better predictors of conflict exist other than the set of internal attributes considered. Variables such as the host country's degree of political stability, economic development, or extent of differences in political and economic ideology of significant constituents could be fruitful variables for future research. The firm's management orientation or philosophy and strategy may also account for this unexplained variation in the dependent variable.

In the following sections, we will explore the differences in management orientations and philosophies of American, European,[d] and Japanese multinationals and their impact on MNC–host country conflicts. This analysis is based on our extensive interviews of executives of 124 MNCs, 50 governmental officials, and other knowledgeable persons in the six countries studied.

MANAGEMENT ORIENTATION AND ITS IMPACT ON MNC–HOST COUNTRY RELATIONSHIPS

Company Efficiency versus System Effectiveness

In general, the U.S. multinationals studied seem to operate with a notion of efficiency that is different from that of their European and Japanese counterparts. To American managers, the cardinal principle of efficiency is the profitable production of quality goods and services at a price the consumer can afford or is willing to pay. This notion was continually reinforced by the home office, which rewarded the subsidiary on the basis of its annual bottom-line performance. Thus, plant productivity, cost of goods purchased, and similar financial indices became the main concerns of the

---

[d]Seventy percent of the European multinationals studied were either from Germany or Switzerland.

overseas manager. The very legitimacy of overseas operations and their subsequent worth were seen in terms of operational efficiency.

In contrast, the Japanese and Europeans measured success or failure not so much in terms of the operational efficiency criteria used by American multinationals, but by system effectiveness, that is, the degree to which their organization was able to adapt to and cope with the external environments (e.g., new control or regulatory mechanisms). In order to accomplish this, they were often willing to sacrifice short-term operational efficiency. Furthermore, the home office often reinforced the policy of long-term effectiveness by stationing an expatriate manager in the country for a substantial period. The manager's role was evaluated, not so much in terms of bottom-line profits, as in terms of the ability to cultivate and maintain a harmonious interaction with officials from the host government and others in the environment. In contrast, most U.S. executives perceived such activities as a "waste of resources," contributing only to a decrease in efficiency and profitability. In fact, American subsidiary managers were rarely asked by the parent organization to cultivate interface and boundary relationships.

In discussing the short-term profit orientation of American multinationals, the managing director of an American subsidiary, a local national, said:

> Americans are interested in taking out their investments in five years and are then willing to let the company decline and die . . . . (They) develop a habit of walking out from a given market at the slightest provocation. They are too temperamental and don't give a damn about understanding host countries' problems and aspirations. What they want is their fair return . . . their ability to get back their investments in five years, and then remit profits to the maximum extent possible.

A European executive in Southeast Asia expressed a similar viewpoint:

> Americans come here on a temporary basis and set up fly-by-night type of operations, and they disappear as fast as they come. We do not come with such intensions. Because of this American attitude, the (U.S. executives) get very annoyed when the government changes policies. We, too, do not like sudden changes in policies, but this is the name of the game and one should adapt to it. (Also see Franko,[26] for similar observations.)

We also observed that European and Japanese executives were given enough leeway and freedom to set their own targets in a given country, while U.S. subsidiary executives were programmed by their headquarters to produce, sell, and make profits at certain levels.

As the managing director of a large American petroleum company lamented:

Those computer kids in New York tell us what to do, when to eat, and when to travel. We have no freedom like the Japanese and Europeans . . . . They must be paid half as much, but carry a lot of decisionmaking power.

Another characteristic displayed by U.S. executives was their misguided notion that they were doing the host nations a big favor by their very presence. If the host nations did not appreciate this fact, they said they would be only too glad to leave, and gleefully watch the nation's downfall. The following quotations from our interviews provide further insights into the workings of the U.S. overseas executive's mind.

The managing director of a large American MNC in Malaysia, pounding his hand on the desk, said:

We came here because they need us. We can help them. This little country and her little people need help, but they must be reasonable, otherwise we will get out of here.

Commenting on the status of his own company, he said:

We are number one in the world in the manufacturing of_____, and I want you to know, and the world to know about this fact, and I want you to tell this to everybody else.

In contrast, a European MNC executive reflected:

We came here to stay for a long time. We have been here a long time, and intend to stay unless ordered out by the host country. Of course, then we must go . . . . We are, after all, their guests.

Franko, in his study of European multinational companies, emphasized this highly adaptable attitude of the European MNCs:

The continental presence was more discreet . . . the flags of the home countries of continental enterprises did not connote ambitions or superpower capabilities to recipient countries.[27]

The overall attitude of Japanese MNCs toward host nations was even more conciliatory than that of the Americans and Europeans. The overall Japanese view was:

We came here as guests, and our nation is small and needs natural resources, as well as foreign trade and investment to survive.

Japanese multinationals generally emphasized their role as contributing to the overall welfare of their host and home countries. They believed that each of them has a national responsibility to secure resources for Japan, to provide opportunities for small manufacturers from Japan to invest overseas, to sell their advanced technology, and to help host nations achieve their own socioeconomic objectives. Of course, such a "collective" orientation, in contrast to the "individualistic" orientation of the U.S. executive, strongly reflects Japan's national heritage and religious beliefs.[28]

Whether such differences among the Americans, Europeans, and Japanese are substantial or not, government officials and opinion leaders (the press and academicians) in the countries studied perceived the existence of such differences. A high-ranking government official in Singapore, a country very cordial to the United States, said:

> Americans are more jumpy, impulsive, and reactive, while Europeans are very conservative and go with a step-by-step approach in decision making. . . Europeans come here to stay, and Americans come on a short-term basis.

Not surprisingly, this attitude was apparent in MNC investment strategy, reaction to changes in host government policies, and the selection and training of overseas managers. This finding is examined in greater detail in the following section.

Adaptive versus Reactive Behavior

Generally speaking, U.S. multinational executives perceived policy changes in the host countries as a substantial threat to their operations. Their usual reaction to change was belligerent. Instead of negotiating discreetly, they preferred to overreact and ignore diplomacy. In the majority of cases studied, they failed to distinguish between an actual governmental policy change and mere shifts in attitude adopted by the host government only to placate political factions within a nation. In certain cases, U.S. MNCs precipitated policy changes by reacting prematurely to inconsequential statements made by the representatives of the host government.

The Japanese, meanwhile, viewed generally the source of their problems with host governments in actions taken by third parties — students, organized labor, consumer groups, and even American multinationals. During times of conflict, they assumed a very low profile and waited for the tension to dissipate.

European executives usually assumed a "philosophical" position on any issue that arose. They blamed neither the government (as Americans did), nor other publics (as the Japanese did). For the most part, they were generally charitable to American MNCs facing specific problems with the host country. In brief, they preferred to stay on the sidelines and were very willing to compromise. As a Swiss executive in Brazil explained:

MNCs should operate within the framework of Eastern philosophies: No public debate, no press releases, no big announcements, no big fanfare, just do the job.

He went on to recommend,

. . .a philosophy of harmony and cooperation instead of raising issues. . ., keeping a low profile, asking no questions, and working within host government policies, and solving problems at a personal level, rather than at the public level.

Similarly, a European executive in Malaysia, referring to a sudden change in that country's investment policies (requiring that a fixed proportion of employees be "Bhumiputras") said:

The government's goals and objectives do change, and we must adapt to these changes. This is what international business is all about; we must constantly adapt to new circumstances, and nobody can say that the government has to keep its goals and policies the same for all time.

With reference to the same policy change, an American executive reacted by saying:

The recent two acts are unconstitutional and amount to illegal takeover of foreign companies. (The government) is tyrannical, and no different from that in other developing countries. . . I will not advise my company to invest any more in Malaysia.

Such differences in MNC behavior patterns and reactions were further revealed by examining the perceived intensity of conflicts, the consequences of conflicts, and the extent of the involvement of senior executives in these episodes.

Table 4-5 shows that of all the conflicts faced by American MNCs, 44 percent were described by their executives as very intense. On the other hand, only 16 percent of the conflicts were rated as less intense by the U.S. executives. The European MNCs were not far behind: 38 percent of their conflicts were described as highly intense. The Japanese MNCs, however, noticeably played down the intensity of their conflicts in the host countries. Only 26 percent of their conflicts were evaluated as highly intense.

The low-profile strategy adopted by the Europeans and Japanese had favorable payoffs in terms of the ultimate consequences of the conflicts. American MNCs had twice as many breakdowns in relationships as the Europeans and three times more than the Japanese. The Europeans and

Japanese apparently prevented their conflicts from ending in dire conse-
qences. (For similar conclusions, see also Franko,[29] Boddewyn and
Kapoor,[30] Heller and Wilatt.[31] The desire of the Japanese MNCs to maintain a low profile is further shown by the relative lack of direct involvement
of their senior personnel in conflict situations.

**Table 4–5. Intensity of Conflict by Origin of Controlling Ownership of
MNC**

	Intensity of Conflict			
Ownership	High N %	Medium N %	Low N %	Total N %
United States	19/44	17/40	7/16	43/100
European	13/38	25/35	9/27	34/100
Japanese	6/26	6/26	11/48	23/100

Source: Author interviews as reported in Anant R. Negandhi and B.R. Baliga, *Quest for Survival
and Growth* (New York: Praeger, and Königstein, West Germany: Athenäum, 1979), p. 47.

Managerial Attributes and Conflict Resolution

In their responses to our question — "What talents do you consider are
most needed by the executive personnel dealing with the host
governments?" — all MNC executives interviewed seemed reasonably in
agreement. All of them ranked interpersonal competence and influential
contacts as the most desirable qualities. In addition, the Japanese MNCs
placed major emphasis on the "political" and diplomatic skills of their
executives.

The American, European, and Japanese executives, however, differed
considerably in applying their resources to conflict resolution. The
American approach, in most cases, was to place all their cards on the table
and to attempt to resolve the problem in the public arena. They appeared to
be under the impression that their interests would be best served through a
general and open discussion of the issues involved. They tried to generate
such a dialogue through press releases, by pressuring government officials
independently, through industry associations, or even through U.S. em-
bassies and consulates.

A European executive in Brazil commented on this approach, and he con-
trasted it with his own (European) approach in this way:

> The American way of bringing things out into the open . . . is stupid. What do
> they achieve? We do not understand the American way . . . . The company
> should be careful not to raise any dialogue or do anything via debate . . . I
> would suggest complete secrecy and solving problems discreetly at the personal
> level.

Another European executive in Malaysia expressed similar thoughts:

> Americans get into conflict with government . . . this is the American way of life. They do not like governments to tell them what to do, and they get on right away (in debate) with the government officials and fight if the officials attempt to control them. This may be the life style in America, and they are used to this life style . . . and think it applies equally here (in host nations).

The host government officials also perceived Americans as aggressive and far too vocal. A Brazilian government official, for example, stated:

> Americans bring out everything in public . . . . We do not understand it. It is okay philosophically, but washing dirty linen in public does not solve anything . . . . we do not understand the American way.

On the other hand, both European and Japanese executives were adept at keeping a low profile, and they did their best not to raise questions in public. They preferred to work discreetly and make very subtle efforts to influence the decisionmakers. In times of stress, they (especially the Japanese) did not hesitate to push their "big brothers" (U.S. MNCs) into the limelight, taking shelter in their shadows.

Responses to Policy Changes

Substantial differences among the three groups of MNCs were clearly reflected in their responses to specific issues and policy changes that were being debated at the time of our study. We examined three policy changes that were announced recently in three countries — Malaysia, India, and Peru — in order to illustrate these differences.

Malaysian Case. The Malaysian government now requires all foreign corporations to increase equity holdings by nationals and also specifies proportions in which various ethnic groups are to be employed in an organization. The required percentages are 30 percent Chinese, Indian, and those of other national origins who are Malaysian citizens; 40 percent Bhumiputras, who are considered to be the "true" Malaysians; and 30 percent foreigners (expatriates).

To implement this policy, the government formed a ministerial committee, which has begun to issue letters of invitation to various foreign companies to appear before the committee and discuss their plans for compliance with the stated policy.

In response to the question, "What would you do if you get a letter of invitation from the committee?" the typical answer of Japanese MNCs was:

We have already done so and implemented this policy of the government in terms of equity requirements, and will attempt to do the same with respect to the employment of the different national groups. Of course, this is somewhat difficult, and time-consuming, but the government understands our problems and is sympathetic.

The European response was:

Fine! We have already made plans and look forward to discussing (them) intelligently with the government officials; we are not scared or afraid; we will make every effort to implement this policy.

In commenting on the fairness of this Malaysian policy, a European expatriate manager echoed this reaction, saying:

The government policy of Malayization is correct. And as a matter of fact, they are trying to tell us "look, MNCs, we like you and would very much like your cooperation here, but we have this problem of inequity which may create troubles and a potential revolution. This is not good for you or us. . . , we do not need revolutions, but to avoid this, we must get down to work and remove this inequity; otherwise, neither you nor we will be here . . . . (To us) this is a realistic situation and we are prepared to work with the government."

In contrast, an American executive's reaction to the same policy was:

These policies are political in nature and will and should not be implemented; but if they are, it will hurt the country and the inflow of foreign investment.

The American executive's response was to make a long distance call to the vice-president of the international division of his company, and then fly home for detailed instructions. The majority of the American expatriate managers interviewed felt that the policy was unconstitutional, and that they would rather pull out than implement it.

In reality, however, neither the Japanese nor the European MNCs in Malaysia had made any serious efforts to increase the employment of "Bhumiputras" in the proportions desired by the government. American MNCs, on the other hand, had a higher proportion of locals on their employee rosters. As we will see in a later section, Europeans and Japanese have been relatively slow in placing local nationals in top-level positions, not only in Malaysia, but also in other developing countries.

Furthermore, American MNCs have shown the greatest reluctance to comply with equity dilution requirements, while the Europeans and Japanese have demonstrated a greater flexibility to do so. The American refusal appears to have placed them in an awkward position, which the host government officials have variously attributed to "American stubbornness, inflexibility, imperialism, and indecisiveness."

The Indian Case. Analogous to the Malaysian case, the Indian governments Foreign Exchange Regulation Act (FERA) of 1973 requires that all foreign equity holdings be diluted to 40 percent, unless the firm is operating in the "priority sector," which is designated from time to time by the government, the firm is exporting at least 65 percent of its production, or both.

Here again, the typical response of European MNCs was to increase their exports to the required amount, dilute their equity, increase investments in the "priority sectors," or one or all of these steps. It was interesting to note, for example, that a well-established European tobacco company (a nonpriority industry) sought the advice of an Indian consulting firm in order to find ways of investing its large accumulated capital in cement manufacturing. When we asked some American executives about this move by the European company, the majority of them felt that the company was "out of its mind." The Americans also felt that if they were to recommend investment in an unrelated but priority industry to their home office, they would be immediately fired or called home and demoted. Accordingly, they spoke more in terms of pulling out of India, or exerting pressure on the Indian government through the U.S. State Department or other U.S. and international agencies.[e]

The Peruvian Case. Similar reactions were observed in Peru with respect to the Andean Pact Regulations, particularly "Decision 24," which requires all foreign companies to become "mixed companies" with 51 percent local ownership within fifteen years.[32] The typical European and Japanese response to this regulation was: "We will do it when the time comes," or "We have already done so." The Americans frequently talked about leaving or putting pressure on the Peruvian and other Andean Pact countries to change these regulations.

Differences in Interpretation. Our extensive interviews further confirmed that the examples described above were not unique. A detailed analysis of the conflict response patterns led us to believe that in interpreting government policies, the Japanese managers were inclined to follow what they called "political instructions," which were communicated orally by government officials or reported in the press, regardless of whether such instructions were spelled out in the policy framework or not. In contrast, the American tendency was to refer to the *documentation* of policies, and to act accordingly. The usual reasoning of American MNCs seemed simple and straightforward:

[e]Two recent cases in which IBM and Coca Cola withdrew from India exemplify this point.

If the governmental policies are favorable to our company's overall interests, we will come (forward to invest) and continue our operations; if they are not, we will not (come forward to invest) and pull out our existing investments.

The actions of an American petroleum company, IBM, and Coca Cola in India and petroleum companies in Malaysia amply illustrate this attitude. In India, one company decided to withdraw its investment in petroleum refining and marketing operations when the Indian government began to implement its petroleum policy of increasing the market share of companies in the public sector. In Malaysia, when the government announced its interim royalty rate (7.5 percent of the total revenue) for oil exploration undertaken by foreign MNCs, an American MNC, which did not agree with the rate, decided to stop its drilling operation. This particular situation in Malaysia generated heated arguments between company and government officials, which also affected other multinationals. In response to a company's reaction to the Malaysian petroleum policy, Mr. Razaleigh, then chairman of the government-owned petroleum company, said:

We are prepared to listen to reason, not threats . . . Petronas (the government-owned company) will not submit to threats of pulling out "huge investments" from Malaysia . . . they must realize that the oil belongs to this country and our people, and we will not allow them to take all our wealth away.[33]

Preference for Clarity in Government Policy. Our interviews also revealed that the American MNCs found it difficult to operate with vague and diffuse policies. As the top executive of an American petroleum company in Singapore explained:

What is important to us is not what the rules of the game are, but their consistency. We can operate under strict controls, or no controls at all . . . but what is terribly difficult is when you gear your approach to certain markets and, all of a sudden, more controls are slapped on overnight, or when you had a tightly controlled situation, and the controls are taken off.

Such preferences for clarity and consistency in policies are natural, for they make life easier for the multinationals. Uncertainties, and changes, however, are a fact of life, particularly in international business, and by and large, American MNCs have reacted poorly to changes in their environment.

The Japanese, on the other hand, viewed unregulated situations as advantageous to them; the lack of specific policies meant that there were no specific constraints with which they had to contend. Whenever clarification was needed, they felt it could be gained by talking to influential persons, government officials, bankers, and their own embassy personnel.

To the Europeans, the existence of confused situations only meant that the world is dynamic. They also felt that if certain policies were too restrictive right now, they would change in time, and that they should be prepared to wait for such eventual changes.

Such insistence on clarity by the U.S. multinationals apparently conveyed an impression of stubbornness and inflexibility to the host government officials, whose own sociocultural background made them tolerant of vagueness.

PERSONNEL POLICIES

American MNC Practices

The personnel policies as well as the overall management system of American MNCs have been acclaimed as the most advanced and sophisticated. This was acknowledged not only by host government officials, educators, and union leaders, but also by executives of the European and Japanese MNCs themselves.

American MNCs have been regarded as fair and equitable in dealing with their employees in terms of providing attractive wages and salaries, fringe benefits, training, and promotion opportunities. Because of such enlightened personnel policies, other industrial and commercial enterprises, including European and Japanese MNCs, have had difficulty in attracting and retaining high-level manpower in the developing countries.

American MNCs were also the first to deal with the widespread demand of the developing countries to localize management of the foreign companies. In our earlier study of fifty-six U.S. subsidiaries in six developing countries, we found no more than two dozen expatriate American managers in these companies.[34] In the present study, we noted the continuation of this trend in the declining use of expatriate managers by U.S. multinationals.

As Table 4–6 shows, the majority of top-level executive positions in the U.S. subsidiaries were filled with local nationals. In fact, in our study we found only one company that did not have any national in a top-level position. In contrast, fifteen Japanese multinationals (78.9 percent) did not employ even one national in top-level management. Table 4–6 indicates that European MNCs had localized their operations considerably more than the Japanese, although to a lesser extent than the American MNCs.

Our study also indicates that Japanese multinationals are more likely to employ Japanese personnel at lower levels, despite the availability of skilled and competent personnel in the host country. It was not uncommon to find that the first-line supervisor in Japanese multinationals were Japanese nationals. Such practices contributed significantly to the operational problems with which the Japanese multinationals were plagued.

Table 4-6. Extent of Localization of Top-Level Management by MNCs

	MNC Ownership		
	U.S.	European	Japanese
Localization of Top-Level Management	(N = 44)	(N = 33)	(N = 19)
	N/%	N/%	N/%
100	12/27.3	3/9.1	0/0
75–99	14/31.8	13/39.4	0/0
51–74	7/15.9	4/12.1	2/10.5
1–50	10/22.7	8/24.2	2/10.5
0	1/2.3	5/15.2	15/78.9

Source: Author interviews.
Chi Square = 53.03.
D.F. = 8
Level of Significance = 0.01.

Japanese MNC Practices

Among the multinationals studied, the Japanese seem to have the most severe problems with their employees. They experienced the greatest difficulty in attracting, retaining, and motivating employees at all levels. Generally, the Japanese MNCs followed two distinctive modes in their personnel policies. The first was to practice the Japanese style of management, in which they would attempt to introduce the Japanese practice of life time employment and promotion based on seniority, with complete employee loyalty demanded by the company. The other mode was to treat the local employees in the same manner they were treated by domestically owned companies. This resulted in maintenance of the status quo, and employees were often held in low esteem as was the custom in many local enterprises and government agencies. Because of rising expectations and a better understanding of the status of workers in other countries, these policies have resulted in low morale, low productivity, and higher absenteeism and turnover rates.[35] Although the expatriate Japanese managers failed to see the causes of their problems, they did admit that they had serious manpower and personnel problems in their operations. (These practices are in sharp contrast with those of the Japanese MNCs in the United States. See Chapters 2 and 3.)

European MNC Practices

In recent years, European MNCs have made considerable strides in catching up with the Americans in their management systems and personnel policies. Although there are still subtle differences in basic orientation, management philosophy, and business practices of American and European companies, the gap between them in regard to their personnel policies for local employees is fast narrowing. Especially at the levels of unskilled and skilled workers and supervisory and middle management, there are no great differences in wages, or in the type of training and promotion opportunities available. As we will discuss later, however, at the higher technical and managerial levels, the American and European companies still differ somewhat.

Background and Career Patterns

The American overseas manager is always on the move. Both occupational and intercompany mobility is a built-in feature of the manager's working life. The usual tenure of a U.S. subsidiary manager in a given position is between three to five years. In our interviews, we found only a handful of American expatriates who had lived in a given country more than five years. Many of them were newcomers who hoped that their assignment overseas would not mean that they had been demoted. Even those who had taken up their assignment less than a year ago expressed a desire to be transferred to the home office again soon.

In contrast, the European and Japanese managers thought of their overseas career as a long-term commitment. They felt that, basically, they were international executives, and they had assumed their present positions to strive for long-term objectives, both for their companies and for themselves. A typical response of a Japanese expatriate manager to the question, "Where do you go next, and when?", was:

> I came here only five years ago, and it will depend upon that man (pointing to the picture of the president of his company), but I came here to stay.

The response of the European executive was the same as that of the Japanese, except that there was no picture to which the executive could point. As one German manager in Malaysia explained:

> This is not quite heaven, but it is a good place to live and raise a family . . . .

Speaking on behalf of all other Europeans, he said:

> We are international executives, and we have, by choice, decided to pursue overseas careers and, unlike Americans, for us the question does not arise where to go next.

The United States is a very mobile nation, and an attitude toward an overseas assignment by the typical U.S. overseas manager like that described above is both realistic and understandable. The contrast among American, European, and Japanese attitudes toward and expectations in their career goals, however, creates an unfavorable image for the American MNCs. Partly because of the short term of their assignments, American overseas managers are thought of by host officials as "second-rate" executives who are not given much decisionmaking power by their headquarters. European and Japanese expatriates, on the other hand, are regarded as influential and important persons who possess high status within their companies. Whether such a situation was true or not, in the eyes of host government officials and leading local businessmen, this was considered to be a fact. Frequently, government officials in developing countries have demanded that U.S. subsidiaries call in their vice-presidents or presidents even for minor discussions, thus implying that expatriate managers are not considered important enough in the management hierarchy, or lack sufficient influence or authority to make important decisions.

Significant differences were also observed in the background and training of American, European, and Japanese executives. As expected, a large majority of the expatriates interviewed were college graduates, although the nature of their studies differed considerably. Approximately two-thirds of the American expatriates were either business or engineering majors, or both. a large majority of Japanese expatriates specialized in international economics and other social sciences. A large number of the European managers, on the other hand, had earned a degree in the humanities and liberal arts.

We found that in another large-scale study, made more than a decade ago of American overseas managers, over 50 percent of the graduates were business or engineering majors, with approximately 44 percent humanities and liberal arts majors.[36] More recently, however, greater emphasis is being placed on business administration education. This is quite evident from the survey of *Fortune 500* chief executives. The study reports that "more than half of today's top officers majored either in business or economics, and more than a quarter studied in graduate school.[37]

In earlier studies by Newcomer[38] and Warner and Abegglen,[39] it was found that less than one-third were business graduates. The *Fortune* survey also reports an increasing trend toward legal and financial training among top executives. The survey states:

> The expanding size and complexity of corporate organizations, coupled with their continued expansion overseas, have increased the importance of financial planning and controls. And the growth of government regulations and obligations companies face under law has heightened the need for legal advice. The engineer and the production man have become . . . less important in management than the finance man and the lawyer.[40]

Our interviews, however, indicated that such a trend, although true for high-level corporate officials, has not yet penetrated to the level of managers of subsidiaries in the developing countries. The emphasis for them is on the "nuts and bolts" part of business, such as bottom-line profits, internal efficiency, and productivity. As mentioned earlier, these executives do not devote sufficient time to interface relationships.[41]

As opposed to the training received by American expatriate managers, European and Japanese managers, both in their formal education and in their in-company training, are indoctrinated to be sensitive to the demands of the external environment. They are very concerned that their organizations be "positioned" in such a way that they do not "stick out like a sore thumb."[42] As discussed earlier, their primary concern was to adapt to the sociocultural environment, whereas the American executives perceived themselves as "change agents." The Americans usually found the socio-economic and political environments in the developing countries hostile and not conducive to the private enterprise system.

The American Dilemma

In spite of the proven superiority of American management practices, and despite the efforts to localize U.S. overseas operations, the personnel policies of the American MNCs are being increasingly criticized by their own employees and by government officials. The apparent slowness of European and Japanese MNCs to place local nationals in responsible positions has, however, been overlooked by the host governments. Why?

Host government officials as well as the top-level local employees interviewed felt that although American companies responded to the desire of the host governments for more local managers, they merely followed the letter of the law and not its spirit. In localizing overseas operations, the critics contend, they have not only withheld decisionmaking powers from local nationals, but also from the remaining expatriate managers. It was also frequently pointed out to us by government officials that the quality of the American expatriate managers was "inferior" to that of their European and Japanese counterparts. Common expressions of host government officials were:

"Americans cannot make decisions . . . ."
"They are too inflexible . . . ."
"They do not have enough power . . . ."

An illustrative and striking example of such an evaluation was reflected in the public demand by a senior Malaysian governmental official that the president or vice-president of a company come from the United States to discuss certain problems. Until that time, the official had declined to grant even a courtesy appointment to the subsidiary manager.

Simultaneously, the presence of a sizeable number of expatriates in the European and Japanese MNCs appears to have been conceived by the host countries in generally positive terms. They have been credited by the host government as possessing substantial decisionmaking power and as being more flexible in their attitudes than the Americans. They are also regarded as having closer ties with their headquarters, and even the ability to influence major decisions affecting subsidiary operations.

Thus, it seems to us that the localization of management by American MNCs has turned out to be a disadvantage for the U.S. companies. Some of the American expatriate managers interviewed felt that it was a mistake by their companies to do so. As one American in Thailand said:

> We should not have done it in the first place, but now we do not know how to go back and bring in more expatriate managers . . . Europeans and Japanese are smart . . . they have not gone too far in this respect.

HEADQUARTER–SUBSIDIARY RELATIONSHIPS

In order to obtain a better understanding of the problems facing the executives of American subsidiaries, we attempted to explore various facets of headquarter–subsidiary relationships and their impact on MNC (subsidiary)–host country relationships.

Interviews with American executives indicated that they felt strongly about their inability to participate in decisionmaking. Many of them admitted that they were little more than "peons" in terms of the hierarchy at headquarters and that communication between them and the head bosses was strictly formal and minimal in nature. At the same time, many of these executives complained a great deal about the excessive demands made by their head offices for reports and data on subsidiary operations. They felt that these reports and data were for the entertainment of the "computer men," and as one American executive in Thailand put it:

> For these whiz kids who are playing around with the figures but really don't know what to do with the data . . . [the] more you supply, [the] more they want . . . and my two (expatriate) assistants and I spend 60 percent of our time in generating reports and data, and I surely hope somebody is using them at least as toilet paper.

In a similar vein, another American expatriate, who had been posted to India after twenty-five years of service at the home office said:

Headquarters demand a lot of documentation from here . . . [but] as far as top brass is concerned, they seem to know very little about what is happening in these countries.

Explaining his relationship with the home office, he pointed out:

We take home leave . . . take a week off to go to our headquarters . . . socialize with the people we know, but communicate with nobody on substantial matters . . . . I sometimes wonder whether the president or even the vice-president of our international division will recognize me . . . . They simply do not care.

Yet another American executive in Thailand echoed his frustration, saying:

I really question whether the top brass at the home office listens to what we say and report . . . I think they are not mature enough to know the conditions prevailing here . . . . We are just beating the drums, nobody cares to listen back home.

And, lastly, a returning American executive who had served for eight years in Malaysia summed up the problems of the U.S. subsidiary–home office relationship. When asked about what report he would have to file on his return regarding his experience abroad, he responded:

I am on my way to San Francisco on my next assignment . . . . They did not call me to report at the head office . . . . If they want to know something about the operation which I started here, they would call me long distance . . . . Hell, they do not need me . . . they know it all!

In contrast to such apparent tension and misgivings between the managers of the U.S. subsidiaries and their head offices, the European and Japanese managers felt very comfortable in their relationship with their head offices. Although there was relatively far less formal reporting in the European and Japanese MNCs, the overseas managers felt that they were involved in and informed about the major strategic decisions undertaken back home and that their own voices and viewpoints were seriously considered in formulating major policies affecting their operations. They also felt they had considerable latitude in running their operations. In this respect, most of the American expatriate managers we interviewed felt that their role and duties were very narrowly defined; they were simply just another cog in the corporate machine.

The rosy picture of the European and Japanese overseas managers just described does not necessarily mean that they did not experience any tension and conflict in dealing with their home office personnel. Yoshino,[43] for example, shows the existence of tension and certain levels of conflict between the Japanese subsidiary and the home office. He ascribes this tension to the unique decisionmaking system that the Japanese employ. This "bottom-up" decisionmaking system is known in Japan as the Ringi system. In underscoring the practical limitations of this system, Yoshino states:

> [The] Japanese have extended the Ringi system of decision-making to international operations with virtually no alterations . . . . [However] the extension of the Ringi system . . . has several immediate as well as long-range implications . . . . First . . . it has created some practical difficulties for the management of foreign subsidiaries, because it is they who must, somehow, bridge the gap that is created by their physical operation and isolation from the parent company. This diverts their attention from the pressing needs of management of the local enterprise and is often a great source of frustration for them. Furthermore, the decision process can be extremely time-consuming when circumstances require rapid responses . . . . [The] long-term implications of extending the Ringi system . . . are that it makes the participation of non-Japanese nationals in the decision-making process extremely difficult.[44]

In criticizing this type of decisionmaking system used in Japanese MNC overseas operations, Yoshino further states:

> Japanese management is a closed, local, exclusive, and highly culture-bound system, and the Ringi system epitomizes it . . . . Compared with the Japanese, the American system is less culture-bound, has greater flexibility, and has a considerable degree of tolerance for heterogeneous elements.[45]

Yoshino's description of the Japanese decisionmaking system is illuminating. In our opinion, however, he has failed to differentiate between the problems created at operation levels, and those at interface levels.

The Japanese do face a great number of operational problems; this may be due to their particular management orientation, including the Ringi system of decisionmaking. Such an orientation, however, has not created problems for the Japanese in dealing with governmental officials in the host countries. As indicated earlier, the officials we interviewed felt that the Japanese managers were much more flexible and had more decisionmaking power than the Americans.

The American system of management was much more advanced, and it was also preferred by employees. But the lack of self-esteem of the managers, coupled with their restricted decisionmaking power and a lack of adequate ocmmunication between the subsidiary and its home office, has caused a large number of interface problems for American MNCs.

The European multinationals overseas appear to be in the best position. Unlike the Japanese, they were not found to be experiencing major operational problems. Although their management system may not be as sophisticated as that of the American MNCs, they are not far behind. Our studies in a number of developing countries indicate that local people would generally rather work for American than European MNCs, owing to their higher wages, better training, and promotion opportunities.[46] Once qualified employees reach higher management positions in the U.S. subsidiaries, they seem to be frustrated with their lack of decisionmaking power and the excessive reporting requirements of their home offices. At this stage, the most able and qualified local employees in the American subsidiaries seek alternative opportunities, either in large local enterprises or in governmental agencies, although there has not been a massive exodus.

In contrast, the European MNCs do not create such high expectations among their local employees initially, but they do promise better job security and a more stable career path. Local nationals do not appear to have as good a chance of reaching top positions in European operations, but at the lower positions they are made to feel important and wanted. Such a feeling of being "wanted" is lacking in the American subsidiaries.

There is little difference between U.S. and European MNCs with regard to their interface conflicts. Our interviews clearly showed, however, that Europeans have learned to adapt better to changing circumstances. In fact, it would not be foolhardy to predict that European MNCs will experience less conflict in the years to come than U.S MNCs (provided that present trends continue), since their flirtation with U.S. management practices seems to be on the wane.[47]

INVESTMENT POLICY AND STRATEGIES

The American, European, and Japanese multinationals all desire to have 100-percent equity holding in their subsidiaries. The Europeans and Japanese, however, appear to have reconciled themselves to the leverage of the host governments and have more readily accepted majority or even minority (especially the Japanese) positions. American MNCs have often made threats of divestiture in order to retain 100-percent equity, and such an attitude has begun to hurt them. Because of this insistence on 100-percent equity, some host governments are bypassing U.S. MNCs whenever large-scale projects are to be developed in the public sector.

Furthermore, U.S. MNCs appear to be reluctant to enter fields in which they do not possess the necessary know-how. Acquisition of know-how through partnership with another American firm is generally not pursued. (In many instances U.S. anti-trust laws discourage such moves.) There is a great concern with the notion of internal efficiency, expressed, for example, in a strong desire to build plants that achieve economies of scale. In contrast to such American policies, the Japanese investment policies are very flexible. If the Japanese had to, they would even settle for minority equity holding, or go into partnership with others, including Japanese trading companies, other Japanese investors, local investors, as well as governmental enterprises. Usually, Japanese overseas investment was undertaken by a large trading company that coordinated its efforts with other firms (generally Japanese) possessing the requisite know-how. In a sense, Japanese trading companies serve as catalysts for Japanese manufacturing investment in Southeast Asia, as well as in Latin America.

Despite their minority equity holding, a significant proportion of the Japanese firms manage to retain management control through the use of various subagreements for raw materials, spare parts, disposal of end products, and so on. The Japanese are also willing to spread their investment over diverse operations. In other words, their limited amount of capital investment was channeled into a number of activities, both to minimize risk and to demonstrate their flexibility to the host country. When questioned by host governments about their contribution to socioeconomic development, they would point out the extensiveness of their involvement and investment, their impact on employment generation, and the variety of products they were manufacturing. In this way, they would stress their intense concern for the socioeconomic development of the host country. When the multinationals would come under fire, however, they would disappear from public view and take an extremely low profile, saying:

> We are not big . . . we are not multinationals . . . we have only small equity holdings, as required by host governments.

In our interviews, large trading companies like Mitsui, Marubeni, Mitsubishi, and others, doing business in the range of $250 to $400 million per year in a given country, claimed that they were not multinationals, while much smaller American manufacturing companies with investments of less than $50,000 would widely advertise their international stature.[48] To cite a typical example, a Japanese company operating in Thailand, with an investment of no more than $1 million, managed to control four textile companies, three steel mills, one food company, one large trading company, and ten other companies with products ranging from tissue paper to metal fabrication. The sales volume of this firm was about $450 million (U.S) per year; and it claimed to provide employment for 10,000 locals. In the same country, a typical American investor would invest about $1.5 million in a single plant providing employment for approximately 300 to 400 employees. Nevertheless, the American company would maintain a high profile, while the Japanese firm would be barely noticeable.

As indicated earlier, we found that the Japanese investor was willing to enter into areas in which the investor's company currently lacked know-how. In other words, the possession of a particular technique or product was not the criterion for overseas investment; it was, in fact, the other way around. Japanese multinationals were generally very receptive to whatever the host government wanted to be done. When the negotiating firm did not possess a technique, it would invite other Japanese or foreign investors to join the firm. The Japanese also showed a willingness to enter into innovative terms of agreement. Such agreements might include providing technology and know-how in return for either long-term raw material supplies or end products for Japanese, European, and American markets.

The European mode of investment fits in between that of the United States and Japan. The European strategy was one of diversification. The Europeans, however, generally preferred to retain a larger proportion of equity than did the Japanese, although their insistence on a 100-percent equity position was not as great as that of the Americans. In addition, the Europeans were not necessarily against entering into joint ventures with host governments.[49]

Thus, our study in the developing countries, unlike our study in an industrialized country — the United States — reveals considerable differences in the management orientations, strategies, and policies of American, European, and Japanese multinational companies.

The implications of these findings from two different but related studies of practicing managers, governmental policymakers, and academic researchers will be examined in the next chapter.

NOTES

1. M. Haire, D.E. Ghiselli, and L.W. Porter, *Managerial Thinking: An International Comparison* (New York: John Wiley, 1966); M.Y. Yoshino, *Japan's Managerial System: Tradition and Challenge* (Cambridge, Mass: MIT Press, 1968); A.R. Negandhi, *Modern Organizational Theory* (Kent, Ohio: Kent State University Press, 1973); A.R. Negandhi, *Interorganizational Theory* (Kent, Ohio: Kent State University Press, 1980); S.M. Davis, *Comparative Management: Cultural and Organizational Perspectives* (Englewood Cliffs, N.J.: Prentice Hall, 1971); G.W. England, *The Manager and His Values* (Cambridge, Mass.: Ballinger Publishing Company, 1975); F.A. Heller, *Managerial Decision Making: A Study of Leadership Styles and Power Sharing Among Senior Managers* (London: Tavistock Publications, 1971).
2. O.H. Nowotny, "American vs. European Management Philosophy," *Harvard Business Review,* Vol. 42, No. 2 (March–April 1964): 101–108.
3. Yoshino, *Japan's Managerial System.*
4. J. Stopford and L.T. Wells, *Managing the Multinational Enterprise — Organization of the Firm and Ownership of the Subsidiaries* (New York: Basic Books, 1972); L.G. Franko, *The European Multinationals* (Stamford, Conn.: Greylock Publishers, 1976); M. Yoshino, Japan's Multinational Enterprises (Cambridge, Mass.: Harvard University Press, 1976); R. Vernon, "Some Tentative Hypotheses on the Behavior of European-Based and Japanese-Based Multinational Enterprises," paper for Conference on Multinational Enterprises, Angelli Foundation, Turin, Italy, June 1971; R. Vernon, *Storm over the Multinationals: The Real Issue* (Cambridge, Mass.: Harvard University Press, 1977).

5. Vernon, "Some Tentative Hypotheses," p. 111.
6. Yoshino, *Japan's Multinational Enterprises,* p. 133.
7. Ibid; p. 141.
8. Franko, *The European Multinationals,* p. 197.
9. Vernon, *Storm over the Multinationals,* op. cit.
10. Franko, *The European Multinationals;* Yoshino, *Japan's Multinational Enterprise;* Y. Tsurumi, *Japanese are Coming* (Cambridge, Mass.: Ballinger Publishing Company, 1976); Stopford and Wells, *Managing the Multinational Enterprise; G.P. Dyas and H.T. Thanheiser, The Emerging European Enterprise: Strategy and Structure in French and German Industry* (London: Macmillan, Ltd., 1976).
11. A.R. Negandhi and B.R. Baliga, *Quest for Survival and Growth: A Comparative Study of American, European, and Japanese Multinationals* (New York: Praeger, and Königstein, West Germany: Athenäum, 1979).
12. Vernon, *Storm over the Multinationals;* R. Vernon, "Some Tentative Hypothesis."
13. J.J. Servan-Schreiber, *The American Challenge* (New York: Athenaeum, 1968).
14. Ibid.
15. Ibid.
16. Stopford and Wells, *Managing the Multinational Enterprise;* Vernon, *Storm over the Multinationals;* Vernon, "Some Tentative Hypotheses."
17. J.P. Curhan, W.H. Davidson, and R. Suri. *Trancing the Multinationals* (Cambridge, Mass.: Ballinger Publishing Company, 1977).
18. Vernon, *Storm over the Multinationals.*
19. W. Skinner *American Industry in Developing Economies* (New York: John Wiley, 1968), p. 273.
20. Indian Investment Centre, *Investing and Licensing in India* (New Delhi: Government of India Publications, 1978).
21. Council of the Americas, *Andean Pact: Definition, Design and Analysis* (New York: Council fo the Americas, 1973).
22. "Malaysia Scares Away Foreign Capital with Rules for Redistributing of Wealth," *Wall Street Journal,* September 22, 1975, p. 1.
23. J.N. Behrman, *Decision Criteria for Foreign Direct Investment in Latin America* (New York: Council of the Americas, 1974), p. 44.
24. A.E. Safarian and J. Bell, "Issues Raised by National Control of the Multinational Enterprise," in P.M. Boarman and H. Schollhammer (eds.), *Multinational Corporations and Governments: Business-Government Relations in an International Context* (New York: Praeger Publishers, 1975), pp. 68–77.
25. U.S. Senate, *Multinational Corporations: Hearings before the Subcommittee on International Trade of the Committee on Finance, United States Senate.* Ninety-Third Congress (Washington, D.C.: U.S. Government Printing Office, 1973).
26. Franko, *The European Multinationals,* p. 225.
27. Ibid., p. 222.
28. K. Kitagawa, "A Review of Modern Management in Japan," *Management Japan,* Vol. 9 (1976): 21.
29. Franko, pp. 219–222.
30. J. Boddewyn and A. Kapoor, "The External Relations of American Multinational Enterprises," *International Studies Quarterly,* Vol. 16 (December 1972); 433–453.
31. R. Heller and N. Willatt, *The European Revenge* (New York: Charles Scribner's Sons, 1975).
32. Council of the Americas, *Andean Pact.*
33. *New Strait Times* (Malaysia), June 27, 1975, p. 1.
34. A.R. Negandhi and S.B. Prasad, *The Frightening Angels: A Study of the U.S. Multinationals in Developing Countries* (Kent, Ohio: Kent State University Press, 1975).

35. A.R. Negandhi, *Management and Economic Development: The Case of Taiwan* (The Hague: Martinus Nijhoff, 1973), pp. 102–108.
36. R.F. Gonzales and A.R. Negandhi, *The United States Overseas Executive: His Orientations and Career Patterns* (East Lansing, Mich.: Michigan State University, The Graduate School of Business Administration, 1967).
37. C.G. Burk, "A Group Profile of the Fortune 500 Executives," *Fortune*, May 1976, p. 173.
38. M. NewComer, *(The Big Business Executive: The Factors that Made Him, 1900–1950* (New York: Columbia University Press, 1950).
39. W.L. Warner and J.C. Abegglen, *Occupational Mobility in American Business and Industry*, (Minneapolis: University of Minnesota Press, 1955).
40. Burk, "A Group Profile," p. 177.
41. J. Boddewyn and A. Kapoor, *International Business — Government Relations* (New York: American Management Association, 1973).
42. Franko, *The European Multinationals*, pp. 220–225.
43. M.Y. Yoshino, "Emerging Japanese Multinational Enterprise," in E.F. Vogel, (ed.), *Modern Japanese Organization and Decision-Making* (Berkeley: University of California Press, 1975), pp. 146–166.
44. Ibid., p. 163.
45. Ibid., pp. 164–165.
46. A.R. Negandhi and S.B. Prasad, *Comparative Management* (New York: Appleton-Century-Crofts, 1971), chs. 7 and 8.
47. Heller and Willatt, *The European Revenge*.
48. Franko, *The European Multinationals*, pp. 218–219; Heller and Willatt, *The European Revenge*, p. 219.
49. Franko, *The European Multinationals*, pp. 121–130.

Chapter 5

Summary and Implications

In this volume, we examined the management orientations, strategies, policies, and practices of German and Japanese subsidiaries operating in the United States, and the management orientations and strategies of American, European, and Japanese subsidiaries in six developing countries: Brazil, India, Peru, Malaysia, Singapore, and Thailand.

As noted in Chapter 1, diverse socioeconomic and political and cultural settings were selected to assess the impact of differing environmental conditions on management strategies, policies, and practices. Our overall aim was to examine similarities and differences in management orientations, strategies, policies, and practices of the American, European, and Japanese multinational corporations in developed versus developing countries. More specifically, the study in the Untied States examined personnel policies, attitudes toward community, nature of decisionmaking and information sharing, time horizons, and the attitudes toward change. It also explored the nature of headquarter–subsidiary relationships, control strategies, and the integrating mechanism used by the German and Japanese subsidiaries.

We also attempted to examine the investment strategies, marketing orientations and practices, and the attitudes and response patterns of these subsidiaries toward the public debate on such issues as foreign imports, dumping practices, competition, and environmental protection legislation.

The study in the six developing countries provided a comparative perspective for the management orientations, strategies, policies, and practices of these two types of multinationals in the developed versus the developing countries. This study also discusses the policies and practices of the American subsidiaries in those countries.

As noted earlier, the results reported in this volume are based on two different but interrelated studies undertaken in the United States and the six developing countries. The former study consisted of seventeen German subsidiaries and sixteen Japanese subsidiaries operating in the United States, while the study in the developing countries was undertaken with 124 subsidiaries of American, European, and Japanese multinational companies.

In this final chapter, after briefly reviewing the main results of our studies, we will pinpoint the implications of our findings.

SUMMARY OF RESULTS

The United States

The study of the German and Japanese subsidiaries in the United States revealed differences in management orientation, particularly in employee relations. The Japanese orientation was considerably more "humanistic," with a greater concern for the employees and the immediate community in which the subsidiaries were located. The Japanese subsidiaries were also relatively more decentralized in their decisionmaking.

The larger size of the German subsidiaries in the United States induced their headquarters to rationalize the production and marketing processes at a global level, quite similar to the practices of large American multinationals. In other words, "mother–daughter" relationships between headquarters and the subsidiary, as practiced in the past by the European multinationals, were abandoned and replaced by a divisionalized structure,[1] while the Japanese multinationals still used the "international association" concept.[2] Japanese subsidiaries were also more deliberate and careful in reacting to disturbances in the environment.[3] There was no difference in time orientation, however. Both German and Japanese subsidiaries operated on a fairly long time perspective.

There were no significant differences in reporting requirements for the German and Japanese subsidiaries. Only a few German subsidiaries were asked to submit their production targets and schedules more frequently.

In terms of power exercised by these subsidiaries in dealing with the regulatory agencies, the German subsidiaries seemed to have a little more leverage because of their greater employment potential (e.g., VW in Pennsylvania threatened the labor union with withdrawing its investments in the United States). Using such leverage, however, was more the exception rather than the rule. Overall, the leverage possessed by both types of subsidiaries was extremely limited.

There were also no significant differences between them in their modes of external relations. Both of them used low key profiles with ad hoc procedures in dealing with the external public. In a few cases, the Japanese subsidiaries used a legal strategy to fight charges of "dumping" and "unfair trade practices."

Both subsidiaries adopted expansionary strategies and stressed marketing parameters, thus suggesting the overwhelming impact of the prevailing competitive market and economic conditions in the United States.

Overall, the study in the United States indicated a relatively minor impact of the managment orientation, headquarter–subsidiary relationship, and other organizational factors on the efficiency of the enterprise in terms of profits and growth, while the market and economic conditions played an important role both in the formulation and implementation of the firm's strategies.

The Developing Countries

As noted in Chapter 4, the main purpose of this part of the study was to examine the conflicts and conflicting issues among the multinational corporations, the host country governments, and other publics in the host countries. Fifty-four American, forty-three European, and twenty-seven Japanese multinationals (subsidiaries) were studied in the six developing countries. By analyzing conflicts and conflicting issues we were able to ascertain the nature of management orientations and strategies, policies, and practices of these three types of multinational corporations.

Briefly, our results indicate that:

1. American and European MNCs tend to have a larger number of interface conflicts[a] in the host countries than the Japanese MNCs.
2. Japanese MNCs tend to have more operational problems than the European and American MNCs.
3. Wholly owned and majority-owned subsidiaries tend to have more interface conflicts than minority-owned subsidiaries.
4. Firms operating in a seller's market or in a moderately competitive market tend to have a larger number of interface conflicts than firms operating in a competitive market.
5. MNCs with larger expectational differences between themselves and the host governments face more interface conflicts than those with smaller expectational differences.

[a]Interface conflicts are conflicts between MNCs and host governments that resulted from negotiational differences, policy differences, or both.

6. The type of industry, number of years in operation, size of its employee force, level of capital investment, level of technology used, and extent of product diversification made a very marginal impact on the MNC's host country relationship.

The content analysis of our intensive interviews with the executives of 124 multinational corporations, 50 governmental officials, and other knowledgeable persons in the countries studied revealed that the three types of multinational corporations (American, European, and Japanese) were not only different in their management orientations but also in their investment strategies, their behavioral responses in resolving conflicts and conflicting situations, and in their personnel and ownership policies.

As reported in Chapter 4, the American MNCs in the six developing countries seemed to operate with a different notion of efficiency than that held by their counterparts, the European and Japanese MNCs. For the Americans, the cardinal principle of efficiency was profitability, thus reflecting the choice of a criterion of success applicable to the competitive markets of the United States and Western Europe.

In contrast, the Japanese and European multinationals measured the success or failure of their operations, not so much in terms of profitability, but more in terms of long-term growth and the development of conducive relationships with the host countries. To achieve these goals, they were willing to sacrifice short-run operational efficiency. Furthermore, their headquarters reinforced these long-term goals by stationing an expatriate manager in a given country for a long time. In addition, the expatriate manager's performance was evaluated in terms of the manager's ability to cultivate and maintain harmonious relationships with the host governments and other publics in the host countries, and unlike the American managers, not in terms of bottom-line profit figures.

For resolving conflicts and responding to policy changes in the host countries, the behavioral modes of these MNCs were quite different. Generally, American executives perceived policy changes as a substantial threat both to their operations and to the private enterprise system. Their usual reaction to policy changes was belligerent, and instead of negotiating discreetly with governmental officials, they preferred to discuss the issues publicly. In contrast, Japanese and European executives assumed very low profiles in dealing with the government and the other publics in the host country and attempted to resolve their problems in the most discreet manner possible.

Needless to say, such differences in behavioral patterns have had a significant impact on the intensity and consequences of conflicts faced by these MNCs. For example, 46 percent of the conflicts of the American MNCs, as described by the executives themselves, were very intensive, while only 26 percent of the conflicts of the Japanese MNCs were regarded as intensive. Although the European MNCs came closer to the American MNCs in the intensity of their conflicts, they differed significantly in the consequences of these conflicts. American MNCs had twice as many breakdowns of relationships with the host countries as compared to the Europeans, and three times more than the Japanese.

The investment pattern also differed among the American, European, and Japanese MNCs. Americans tend to invest large amounts of money in a single enterprise, manufacturing a narrow range of products, while the European and the Japanese are more diversified both in their product lines and in their investment portfolio. This situation is contrary to the investment pattern in their home countries, in which the U.S. MNCs are more diversified than the Europeans.[4]

Both the Europeans and the Japanese were more willing to accept a joint venture agreement and minority controlling interest in the enterprise, while the Americans remained steadfast in demanding either 100-percent equity and control or majority equity and control. The Europeans and Japanese were also less adamant about going into joint venture relationships with government-owned enterprises.

The American subsidiaries enjoyed much less autonomy in decision-making than the Europeans and Japanese. The headquarter–subsidiary relationships in the American MNCs were also much more formalized and required extensive reporting, while for the European and Japanese MNCs, personal and informal relationships between personnel at headquarters and the subsidiaries played an important role.

Judging from the management orientations, investment strategies, and ownership and control policies of the American, European, and Japanese MNCs in the United States and in the six developing countries, the three types of multinationals are pursuing different modes of global strategies. The American MNCs seem to pursue global rationalization policies in both the industrially developed and the developing countries, while the European (in our case German MNCs) and Japanese MNCs seem to use different strategies and policies in the developed versus the developing countries.

As discussed in Chapters 2 and 3, the German and Japanese subsidiaries in the United States, although still enjoying relatively more autonomy in decisionmaking, are moving toward rationalization of their production and marketing processes with global perspectives. In other words, as seen from the level of centralization in decisionmaking and the relative influence of headquarters and the subsidiaries in major policy decisions, the quest for global rationalization has caught on. The German MNCs are fast catching up with the U.S. MNCs in their pursuit of the global reach, while the Japanese, although stumbling occasionally, are not far behind. Thus, both of these MNCs are more prone to react to the market forces in the United States, while in the developing countries the nonmarket forces (governmental regulations and policies and political factors) have more influence on their strategies and policies. To put it differently, for the European and

Japanese MNCs, business ideology is a conditional phenomenon, while for American enterprise, it is a pure and uncompromisable element. To use the cliché of cross-cultural adaptation, the European and Japanese MNCs are not only "doing in Rome what the Romans do" but are adapting their strategies and policies as to what "the Romans are demanding in Rome." The American MNCs, meanwhile, are sticking to their guns, which they believe is the right and proper thing to do. It can indeed be argued that the strengths of the European and Japanese MNCs operating overseas lie in this area vis-à-vis the American MNCs.

To be sure, as we discussed in Chapters 2 and 3, although the German and Japanese subsidiaries in the United Sates are more centralized in their decisionmaking and are moving toward the global perspective and global rationalization of their production and marketing processes, they still maintain some of the "traditional" management methods and styles that have proven effective for their operations back home and elsewhere. In particular, their attitudes, policies, and practices concerning employees, community, and the government are still distinctively their "own" and different from those of the American MNCs. Overall, they are more oriented to people and the community; they regard government as legitimate and readily accept the right of the government to intervene and interfere in their business operations.[5]

For example, Mr. Dieter Zur Loye, a group vice-president of the American Hoechst Corporation, seems to have reflected the practices and policies of many European and Japanese companies operating in the United States and elsewhere in these words: "We want to be known as a good place in which to work, with good secure jobs. We want to give every employee the feeling that if he or she works well and is loyal to the company, the company will be loyal to him even until he dies."[6] Commenting on social and community responsibilities, Mr. Zur Loye states: "We are not here just to maximize profit, but feel there are some things we can do better. We would not try to maximize profit by paying lower wages or cutting corners on environmental safeguards. We see success as building up a long-term propositon . . . our research director says his prime objective is to improve the lot of mankind and I believe him."[7]

Notwithstanding such differences in attitudes, policies, and practices for the German, Japanese and American MNCs, our results, which are discussed in Chapters 2 and 3, show that the technological, market, and economic imperatives in the Untied States are pushing both the German and the Japanese companies, especially the Germans, toward global rationalization of their production and marketing processes. To put it simply, a convergence in management strategies and policies seems to be occurring. The implications of such convergence, however, have not as yet captured the attention of academic researchers, governmental decisionmakers, and business executives. In the remainder of this chapter we will briefly raise some of the tentative questions about the implications of such convergence for management strategies, policies, and practices.

IMPLICATIONS

Viewed from the perspective of contingency theory, the convergence in multinational strategies, policies, and practices is an entirely logical step, since the contingency theory postulates that the organizational structure and processes should be in congruence with environmental demands.[8] As such, our study indicates that the German and Japanese subsidiaries in the United States are moving toward the American practice of centralization of decisionmaking at headquarters.

It should be noted, however, that there is a considerable time lag in the organizational adaptation process. Like human beings, organizations resist change, and consequently, once strategies, policies, and practices are formulated they are used despite different environmental demands that require different types of organizational responses. For example, it took about twenty-five years for the European MNCs to change their organizational structure to the American style of multidivisional structures. And until 1972, only 70 percent of the European companies on the Fortune list of the 200 largest non-American industrials had changed to a divisionalized structure, although the move is clearly in this direction.[9] The vital question is whether such changes in the organizational structure and decisionmaking process are systematic and are based on a rational kind of logic or are they an ad hoc, "follow the leader" strategy and "shot in the dark" phenomenon disguised in scientific jargon?

FAST CHANGING CONDITIONS IN INDUSTRIALIZED COUNTRIES

Although many of the industrialized countries are operating as "free and open markets" and are generally very congenial to foreign investors, lately they too have begun to question the utility of unchecked foreign investment. In other words, governmental decisionmakers as well as other public groups (labor unions, consumer advocates, and environmentalists) are discovering that national needs, ambitions, and objectives can be at variance with the objectives, goals, and strategies of the MNCs.

The range, nature, and intensity of these issues, of course, differ considerably from country to country, depending upon the prevailing political climate and economic conditions (unemployment, inflation, balance of payments position) and the level of industrial and economic development. For example, in a study of MNCs in developed countries, Fry[10] reported that the issue of worker participation ("Mitbestimmung") was most prominent in West Germany, and traditional issues such as providing new technology, employment, upgrading wages, and developing local resources were considered secondary by government officials.

In contrast, in Belgium the major issues pertaining to MNC activities were related to employment capabilities, potential effect on balance of payments position, research and development activities (lack of), development and utilization of local resources, and worker participation in management. Simultaneously, however, MNCs emphasized their importance in terms of increasing the entrepreneurial spirit, providing new technology, and making consumer goods available at lower prices. These differences in expectations between government and MNC priorities are clearly shown in Table 5-1.

Table 5-1. Expectational Differences Between MNCs and Nation-States

	Germany	
Impact	*Government Wants More*	*Firms Give More*
Worker participation	X	
Increase competition		X
Capital inflows		X
Increase skilled employment		X
Create entrepreneurial spirit		X

	Belgium	
Impact	*Government Wants More*	*Firms Give More*
Increase general employment	X	
Increase skilled employment	X	
Balance of payment effects	X	
Increase R & D efforts	X	
Develop local resources	X	
Worker participation	X	
Worker awareness	X	
Increase quality of consumer services	X	
Social and cultural values		X
Increase entrepreneurial spirit		X
Provide new technology		X
Create lower prices		X

Source: David E. Fry, "Multinational Corporations–Host Government Relationships: An Empirical Study of Behavioral Expectations," D.B.A. dissertation, Kent State University, 1977.

Particularly since the oil crisis of 1973, most of the industrialized nations have experienced a downturn in their economic growth and prosperity, which in turn has created considerable hostility not only toward foreign multinationals but also among the opposing groups in a given society (management against labor, multinationals against foreign multinationals, and multinationals against their own subcontractors). For example, faced with the declining sales of U.S. automobiles, all three of the big U.S. auto companies (G.M., Ford, and Chrysler) have begun to denounce auto imports from Japan and European countries and have asked the U.S. Congress and the president to help them. At the same time, their own subcontractors have publicly accused the auto companies of being "double talkers" by asserting that "it is not just imported cars, it's imported parts that [are] causing problems."[11] The growing complaints about Detroit's policy of importing parts for domestically assembled cars have now reached Washington. Consequently, congressional proposals that were originally designed to limit imports of autos are being amended to place restrictions on imported parts as well.[12]

The results of our own large-scale study reported in Table 5–2 illustrate the nature of demands made by the multinational companies in West Germany, United Kingdom, Spain, Portugal, and France.[b]

As Table 5-2 shows, economic stagnation, triggered by the oil crisis, has generated traditional economic demands even in the more industrialized nations of the world. Except for Spain and Portugal, however, the European countries, where our field research was undertaken, have not yet legislated these demands as the developing countries have done.

One thing appears clear: the less economically developed a country, the more intensive the economic problems, or both, the more demands are placed on multinational corporations and the more willing the country is to legislate these expectations.

Table 5–3 shows the problems faced by the American, German, and Japanese MNCs in various industrialized countries. The labor force seems to be the source of almost half the problems faced by the multinationals. U.S. and German subsidiaries, however, have proportionately more labor problems than Japanese companies, although the underlying theme of labor–management problems is quite different in the various countries. In Germany, for instance, industry representatives were involved in challenging the constitutional validity of the "codetermination" laws and were influencing the election of representatives who were against these laws. The U.S. multinational subsidiaries, owing to stipulations in the law about the size of the workforce, were most susceptible to the laws. Given the confrontational nature of management–labor relations in the United States, American multinationals initially had a difficult time in accepting a collaborative philosophy.

Outside Germany all multinationals, especially the larger U.S. and German multinationals, have been the targets of labor unions oriented toward a leftist idiology. This has been particularly true of Spain and

---

[b]The results of this large-scale study will be reported in the companion volume.

Table 5-2. Nature of Demands Made on MNCs in Selected Industrialized Countries

	Germany (N/%)	United Kingdom (N/%)	Spain (N/%)	Portugal (N/%)	France (N/%)	Total (N/%)
Technology transfer	0/0.0	2/21.4	0/0.0	0/0.0	0/0.0	3/5.3
Exports	0/0.0	1/7.1	0/0.0	0/0.0	1/12.5	2/3.5
Employment	0/0.0	2/14.3	0/0.0	0/0.0	0/0.0	2/3.5
Economic development	3/23.1	5/35.7	10/90.9	9/81.8	7/87.5	34/59.6
Ambivalent	1/7.7	0/0.0	0/0.0	0/0.0	0/0.0	1/1.8
No specific demands	9/69.2	3/21.4	1/9.1	2/2.18	0/0.0	15/26.3
	13/22.8	14/24.6	11/19.3	11/19.3	8/14.0	57/100

Source: Interview data collected by the authors.

Table 5–3. MNCs' Problems in Industrialized Countries

	Host Government (N/%)	Labor (N/%)	Political Groupings (N/%)	Local Competitors (N/%)	Multiple Sources (N/%)	No Problems (N/%)	Regional Economic Grouping (N/%)	Total
U.S. MNCs	1/25.0	11/40.7	1/100.0	1/100.0	1/100.0	8/38.1	0/0.0	23/100
	1/4.3	11/47.8	1/4.3	1/4.3	1/4.3	8/34.8	0/0.0	
German MNCs	0/0.0	12/44.4	0/0.0	0/0.0	0/0.0	3/14.3	0/0.0	15/100
	0/0.0	12/80.0	0/0.0	0/0.0	0/0.0	3/20.0	0/0.0	
Japanese MNCs	3/75.0	4/14.8	0/0.0	0/0.0	0/0.0	10/47.6	2/100.00	19/100
	3/15.7	4/21.0	0/0.0	0/0.0	0/0.0	10/52.6	2/10.5	
Total	4/100	27/100	1/100	1/100	21/100	2/100	2/100	57/100
	4/7.0	27/47.4	1/1.8	1/1.8	1/1.8	21/36.8	2/3.5	

Source: Author interviews

Portugal, where rising nationalistic expectations have made the issue even more difficult to handle. To some extent, the Japanese multinationals appear to have avoided serious problems with labor, owing to their smaller size and their willingness to go into joint ventures with either government organizations or private entrepreneurs. This finding is interesting because, despite being involved in joint ventures or minority holdings in the developing countries, Japanese organizations have had considerable problems with labor.[13] These problems stemmed mainly from historical factors and efforts by the Japanese to impose their management style on workers. It appears that the Japanese multinationals have learned from their experience in the developing countries of Asia and South America, and they have restricted the use of the Japanese management style (such as lifetime employment and demanding loyalty to the company) in the industrialized countries.

Japanese subsidiaries were involved, however, in conflicts with the EEC commission. Problems were centered around charges of "dumping" by Japanese organizations, despite the fact that the accused Japanese companies had manufacturing subsidiaries in the EEC countries. The Japanese organizations responded by adopting a legalistic stance while simultaneously emphasizing their local manufacturing activities in efforts to make the "dumping" charge appear untenable.

As noted earlier, although the industrially developed countries have, thus far, constrained themselves in enacting limiting legislation against foreign private investment and multinational corporations, the public debates and discussions are moving closer to this end at a faster speed than could have been anticipated. For example, the recent establishment of the Foreign Investment Review Agency in Canada,[14] in which pronouncements are made about expected corporate behavior, as seen in Table 5-4, comes very close to what the developing countries have been demanding from foreign investors during the 1960s and 1970s.

Turning to the United States, as unemployment and inflation continue to undermine the people's confidence in national economic conditions, legislators, both at the state and national levels, have begun to introduce legislation to curb the activities of foreign investors and multinational companies. For example, in the last few years approximately half of the fifty states in the United States have introduced legislation to restrict foreign investments in agricultural lands. As mentioned earlier, at a lesser end the subcontractors of U.S. automobile companies as well as the labor unions have begun to question the virtue of multinational investments and their general strategies of global rationalization.

Our findings in the United States, on the other hand, clearly show the increasing trend toward global rationalization and centralization in decision-making. Thus, the question should be asked whether or not the German and Japanese multinationals are flexible enough to turn the tide and maintain their organic structures, as they have been able to do in the developing

Table 5-4. Canada's 12 Good Corporate Behavior Principles (as they relate to alleged objectionable U.S. subsidiary policies)

Guiding Principle Summary	*Alleged Objectionable Practices*
1. Full realization of the company's growth and operating potential in Canada.	1. U.S.-based corporate planners institute expansion and cutback plans without regard for Canada's plan and aspirations.
2. Make Canadian subsidiary self-contained, vertically-integrated entity with total responsibility for at least one productive function.	2. The Canadian subsidiary is primarily an assembler of imported parts or distributor of goods produced elsewhere so operations can be easily shut down or transferred.
3. Maximum development of export markets from Canada.	3. Filling export orders to third-country markets from the U.S. country stock earns credits for U.S. balance of payments rather than Canada's.
4. Extend processing of Canada's raw materials through maximum number of stages.	4. Have as few materials-processing stages as possible in Canada to minimize political leverage.
5. Equitable pricing policies for international and intracompany sales.	5. Negotiated or spurious prices by Canadian–U.S. subsidiaries are designed to get around Canadian income taxes.
6. Develop sources of supply in Canada.	6. Preference for United States or third-country sources for purposes of corporate convenience or political leverage.
7. Inclusion of R&D and product development.	7. The concentration of R&D and product design in the United States means Canada can never develop these capabilities.
8. Retain substantial earnings for growth.	8. Profits earned in Canada do not stay to finance Canadian expansion.
9. Appointment of Canadian officers and directors.	9. Use of U.S. officers and directors to prevent development of local outlook in planning and execution.
10. Equity participation by Canadian investing public.	10. Creation of wholly owned subsidiaries denies policy determination and earnings to Canadians.
11. Publication of financial reports.	11. Consolidation of Canadian operating results into parent company statement or failure to publish any relevant information.
12. Support of Canadian cultural and charitable institutions.	12. Failure locally to support such causes as the United Appeal where parent corporations give generously to comparable U.S. campaigns.

Source: David J. Ashton, "U.S. Investments in Canada: Will the Other Shoe Drop?" *Worldwide P & I Planning* (September–October 1968): 57.

countries, once the circumstances demand them to do so in the industrialized countries?

Even the American multinationals, champions of evolving progressive organizational structures for managing expanding international business (from export department to international division, regional structure, worldwide product setup, and the matrix system),[15] have been warned about the swiftly changing environmental conditions in both the developed and the developing countries.

Business International,[16] a reputable consulting firm in international business, recently identified some of the major economic and political changes that will affect the need for changes in present organizational forms utilized by American and other multinational companies.

Declining or Stagnant Economic Growth in the Industrialized Countries

On the average, Canada, France, West Germany, Japan, the United States, and the United Kingdom will experience a drop in the growth of the GNP from about 3 percent in 1979 to 1 percent in 1980. (For the United States GNP growth may drop from 2 percent in 1979 to 1.25 percent in 1980). The respective figures for other countries from 1979 to 1980 are: Japan, 6.0 to 4.75 percent; West Germany, 3 to 2 percent; Canada, 2.75 to 1.5 percent; and the United Kingdom, 0.5 to 2 percent.[17] While the growth rates in major industrialized countries are declining, inflation continues to soar. Thus, the poorer the future outlook and the higher the inflation rates, the more protectionist forces may be reinforced in the United States and other developed countries.[18]

Declining Growth in Productivity and a Drop in Real Wages

As noted in Chapter 1, during the last decade the United States recorded the lowest rate of productivity growth of any major industrial nation. This lower growth rate, coupled with increasing demands by the labor unions for higher wages, will further increase the tension in labor–management relations. Under such circumstances, the U.S. government will be compelled to exercise greater control over wages, prices, and imports, which in turn may seriously undermine the effectiveness of the global rationalization policies of the multinational companies.[19]

Given such changing economic and political conditions, Business International predicts that the multinational corporations will have to create a responsive organizational structure that will be able to combine the centralization of strategies and policies with increasing decentralization of subsidiary operations.[20]

Whether the German and the Japanese companies, in their quest to adopt the American model of global rationalization, will be able to achieve a marriage between centralization of strategies and policies (as required by the global rationalization concept) and the needed decentralization or higher autonomy of the subsidiary operation is still an open question.

NOTES

1. L.G. Franko, "The Move Towards Multidivisional Structure in European Organizations," in S. Davis (ed.), *Managing and Organizing Multinational Corporations* (New York, Pergamon Press, 1979), pp. 380–397.
2. M.Y. Yoshino, "Emerging Japanese Multinational Enterprises," reproduced in Stanley M. Davis (ed.), *Managing and Organizing Multinational Corporations* (New York, Pergamon Press, 1979), pp. 474–494.
3. See Chapter 2, p. 13.
4. L.G. Franko, *The European Multinationals* (Stamford, Conn.: Greylock Publishers, 1976).
5. T.M. Rohen, "Europeans in America Practice 'Foreign' Management," *Industry Week*, January 22, 1979, pp. 64–67.
6. Ibid., p. 65.
7. Ibid., p. 67.
8. P. Lawrence and J.W. Lorsch, *Organization and Environment: Managing Differentiation and Integration* (Homewood, Ill.: Richard D. Irwin, 1969).
9. L.G. Franko, "The Move Towards Multi-Divisional Structure," op. cit., p. 381.
10. D.E. Fry, *Multinational Corporations*-Host Government Relationships: An Empirical Study of Behavioral Expectations, DBA dissertation, Kent State University, 1977.
11. *Wall Street Journal*, May 14, 1980, p. 1.
12. Ibid.
13. A.R. Negandhi and B.R. Baliga, *Quest for Survival and Growth: A Comparative Study of American, European, and Japanese Multinationals.* (New York: Praeger, and Königstein, West Germany: Athenäum, 1979). ch. 2.
14. A.E. Safarian and J. Bell, "Issues Raised by National Control of the Multinational Enterprise," on P.M. Boarman and H. Schollhammer (eds.), *Multinational Corporations and Governments: Business-Government Relations in an International Context* (New York: Praeger Publishers, 1975), p. 74.
15. J. Stopford and L.T. Wells, *Managing the Multinational Enterprise — Organization of the Firm and Ownership of the Subsidiaries* (New York: Basic Books, 1972).
16. *Business International*, January 4, 1980.
17. Ibid., p. 2.
18. Ibid., p. 7.
19. Ibid., pp. 7–8.
20. Ibid.

Definition and Operationalization
of Variables

DEFINITIONS AND OPERATIONALIZATIONS OF VARIABLES: THE U.S. STUDY

1. *Ownership* was categorized on the basis of the home country of the parent: that is, German and Japanese.

2. *Size* was measured on the basis of
   a. level of investment: average over most recent 5-year period or since commencement of operations if the period of operations in the United States was less than 5 years.
   b. sales revenues: average over the most recent 5-year period or since commencement of operations in the United States if period of operations was less than 5 years.
   c. employee size: average over the most recent 5-year period or since commencement of operations in the United States if period of operations was less than 5 years.

3. *Period of subsidiary operations* was operationalized on the basis of number of years operating in the United States.

4. *Diversification* was operationalized on the basis of the proportion of sales in each SIC category.

5. *Management Orientation* was defined as the sum of values possessed by corporate top management that governs the engagement of the organization with its environment. This was operationalized in terms of the degree to which management was materialistic or humanistic.

6. *Headquarters–Subsidiary relationships* denote the processes employed for monitoring and evaluating subsidiary performance and the degree to which decisions are delegated to subsidiary levels. This was operationalized through computing a delegation index, reporting requirements, and degree of bureaucratization.

7. *Leverage* denotes the bargaining power possessed by the subsidiary and the various units in the environment with which it interacts. Operationalized through an assessment of the resources possessed by the subsidiary, the need for such resources and the number of substitutes available, and the importance of the subsidiary to the total MNC system.

8. *Strategy* denotes the objectives and goals set by the organization and the activities undertaken to achieve them. Operationalized through determining the pattern in the stream of decisions undertaken by the company and categorized as (a) expansionary, (b) maintenance, (c) rescue, and (d) harvesting.

9. *Stance* denotes the position adopted by the subsidiary vis-à-vis members of its environment in the process of implementing strategy. Categorized into one of four stances: (a) confrontational, (b) accommodative, (c) courting, (d) neutral or businesslike.

10. *External relations* denote the mode employed by the organization in maintaining contact with host government representatives and significant members of their environment. Categorized as: (a) personal, (b) collective, or (c) legal on the basis of whether external relations were maintained primarily through personal contact by executives and representatives of the company, through trade associations, or through the use of lawyers and law firms.

11. *Organizational performance* was assessed in terms of (a) efficiency and (b) effectiveness. Efficiency measures were basically input–output measures whereas effectiveness was assessed on the basis to which the organization met the demands of various groups or members of its environment.

DEFINITIONS AND OPERATIONALIZATION OF VARIABLES: THE STUDY IN THE SIX DEVELOPING COUNTRIES

1. *Ownership* was simply categorized as American, European, and Japanese on the basis of the origin of the parent company.

2. *Size* was measured on the basis of the level of the subsidiary's investment, sales volume, number of employees, and on the executive's perception of the relative size of the operation in a given country.

3. *Industry group.* Four industrial categories were created: (a) extractive and mining; (b) chemicals and pharmaceuticals; (c) consumer durables; (d) consumer nondurables.

4. *Period of MNC (subsidiary) operation.* Three categories were created on the basis of the number of years in operation: (a) 15 years or more; (b) 6 to 14 years; (c) fewer than 6 years.

5. *Ratio of equity holding.* Three categories were created: (a) wholly owned; (b) majority owned, if the equity holding by the parent firm in a subsidiary was more than 50 percent; (c) minority owned, if the equity holding was less than 50 percent.

6. *Level of diversification.* Three categories were created: (a) high diversification (more than five distinct products or services); (b) intermediate diversification (less than five, but more than two distinct products; (c) low diversification (less than two distinct products).

7. *Level of technology used.* Executives were asked to rate the level of technology used in their respective firms, relative to the technologies used by the other industrial firms in a particular country, in terms of the following three categories: (a) advanced or sophisticated technology; (b) intermediate technology; (c) low technology. The rationale for using the executives' ratings for this variable is based on our contention that different countries interpret degrees of sophistication of technology differently, based on the countries' own levels of technological and industrial development.

8. *Market competitiveness.* Three categories were created on the basis of the nature of market competitiveness the firm faced in a given country: (a) highly competitive; (b) moderately competitive; and (c) a seller's market.

9. *Market power.* Three categories were created on the basis of the market share of the firm for its main products: (a) strong (market share more than 60%); (b) intermediate (market share 26 to 59%); (c) weak (market share less than 26%).

10. *Market orientation.* The firms were grouped on the basis of their end product sales, namely: (a) exporting to their own parent company, other subsidiaries or both; (b) exporting to third parties overseas; (c) selling to local consumers.

11. *Expectation differences.* The variable was measured through the mean score differences between the responses of the executives and the government officials to a series of questions intended to measure the relative strength of expectation for each item listed.

12. *Home and host country relationships of the MNCs.* This was evaluated by the executives on a nine-point scale, ranging from very cordial to volatile and hostile. Their evaluation was also supplemented with other information collected through interviews with government officials and news reports of various events reflecting home–host relationships.

13. *Conflict.* The nature and degree of conflict was classified into four categories: (a) value conflict; (b) negotiational conflict; (c) policy conflict; (d) operational conflict.

Appendix B

Interview Guide and Questionnaire
Used for the Study in the United States

INTERVIEW GUIDE

Part A

SUBSIDIARY DATA

1) Name of the Company: _____

2) Name of Executive providing information: _____

3) Title of Executive providing information: _____

4) Average net assets (most recent 3-year average): U.S. $_____

5) a. Average gross sales (most recent 3-year average):
                                                U.S. $ _____

    b. Average return on sales (most recent 3-year average):
                                                U.S. $ _____

    c. Average return on investment (most recent 3-year average
        with net assets as base):   U.S. $ _____

6) Average sales revenues per employee: $ _____

7) Percentage average equipment utilization (please circle to nearest
    10%):

    0   10   20   30   40   50   60   70   80   90   100
    _____

8) Primary Product(s)/Service(s) (Please list top 3 in order of
    percentage contribution to sales)

        1. _____|_____   Percent contribution to sales.

        2. _____|_____   Percent contribution to sales.

        3. _____|_____   Percent contribution to sales.

9) Two Digit SIC Classification.

10) Pattern of ownership (please check appropriate box)

        _____ wholly owned by parent
        _____ parent has majority interest
        _____ parent has minority but controlling interest
        _____ parent has minority and non-controlling interest

11) Year of establishment of U.S. operations: _____

12) PERSONNEL PRACTICES

    a. Percentage of expatriates in top level management   81-100 61-80 41-60 21-40 0-20

    b. Percentage of expatriates in middle management   81-100 61-80 41-60 21-40 0-20

    c. Percentage of expatriates in lower/tech management   81-100 61-80 41-60 21-40 0-20

    d. Percentage of TCNs in top level management   81-100 61-80 41-60 21-40 0-20

    e. Percentage of TCNs in middle management   81-100 61-80 41-60 21-40 0-20

    f. Percentage of TCNs in lower/tech management   81-100 61-80 41-60 21-40 0-20

    g. Average number of people sent to headquarters for training/familiarization _____.

    h. Average time spent at headquarters _____.

13) To what extent do you use the following means to maintain the relationship with:

    CODE: 5 = A very great deal   4 = Quite a bit
            3 = Somewhat   2 = A little
            1 = Very little or not at all

		Government Agencies	Significant Groups/Organizations (e.g., Labor) in the host environment

		1	2	3	4	5	1	2	3	4	5
a)	Personal contact by the top level executives										
b)	Personal contacts through the public relations department personnel										
c)	Contact through the legal department										
d)	Collective contact via trade associations (i.e., Chamber of Commerce)										
e)	Contact through press-releases										
f)	Outside lawyers										
g)	Other means: please specify										

14) a) The amount of strategic information provided by headquarters to subsidiary management is

1	2	3	4	5
minimum		moderate		extensive

b) The amount of strategic information provided by subsidiary to headquarters is

1	2	3	4	5
minimum		moderate		extensive

15) How are the operations in this subsidiary organized?

16) To what extent does your subsidiary rely on written policies (from headquarters) to guide its decision-making?

1	2	3	4	5
very little	little	to some extent	quite a bit	very extensive

17) The number of manuals governing decision-making are

1	2	3	4	5
few				many

18) To what extent does your subsidiary use manuals or procedures prescribed by headquarters to guide its decision-making?

1	2	3	4	5
very little	little	to some extent	quite a bit	very extensive

19) How many times did headquarter personnel visit your subsidiary in 1976?

No. of visits	Dominant hierarchical position of visitors	(Code as indicated below)
_____	_____	

1 = Headquarter top management,   2 = division heads,
3 = functional heads,   4 = Headquarter staff,
5 = division, functional staff,   6 = service personnel, etc.

20) What was the nature of these visits in 1976? (open question)

Predominantly ad hoc meetings   ☐

Predominantly regularly scheduled meetings   ☐

21) What corporate level committees, advisory councils, task groups, etc., are representatives from subsidiary members of?

Committee	Purposes of Committee	Ad hoc or standing committee
_____	_____	_____
_____	_____	_____
_____	_____	_____

22) In a typical business month, how often do you have personal contacts with managers in headquarters by means of telephone, telex, or letter? (question refers to head of subsidiary)

Every day	Every other day	Every week	Every other week	Every month
5	4	3	2	1

23) Employing the scale indicated below, please indicate how often your subsidiary sends a report to headquarters containing the following information.

1	2	3	4	5
not at all	yearly	quarterly	monthly	weekly or more frequently

Balance Sheet ☐

Profit and loss statement ☐

Production output ☐

Market Share ☐

Cash and credit statement ☐

Inventory levels ☐

Sales per product ☐

Performance review of personnel ☐

Report on local economic and political conditions ☐

24) How much influence does corporate headquarters and your subsidiary management respectively have on the following sets of decisions?

Check columns for HQ and SUB according to the following scale

1 = very little or no influence
2 = little influence
3 = medium influence
4 = high influence
5 = very high influence

Decisions	HQ						SUB				
	1	2	3	4	5		1	2	3	4	5
a Your borrowing from local banks or financial institution											
b Use of cash flow in your SUB											
c Extension of your credit to one of your major customers											
d Choice of public accountant											
e Introduction of a new product on your local market											
f Pricing on products sold on your local market											
g Servicing of products sold											
h Use of local advertising agency											
i Expansion of your production capacity											
j Determining aggregate production schedule											
k Maintenance of production facilities at SUB											
l Appointment of chief executive of your SUB											
m Use of expatriate personnel from headquarters											
n Layoffs of operating personnel											
o Personnel training program for your SUB											

25) Please trace through for me the development and growth of the subsidiary since its establishment, emphasizing, if possible, the last five years.

26) Could you describe the direction in which this company will move in the future (next five years or so) and measures adopted by you to do so?

27) Every organization has to deal with a number of groups in its environment. At times the objectives of these groups do not coincide with those of the organization. Could you describe any such situations in which you may have found yourself and steps taken to deal with these?

Part B

Please give your opinions regarding the following statements by checking the appropriate scale selection. The two scales that have been employed and their key are as follows:

Agree-Disagree Scale	Influence Scale
VSA – very strongly agree	VC – very considerable
SA – strongly agree	C – considerable
SLA – slightly agree	FC – fairly considerable
SDA – slightly disagree	FL – fairly limited
SD – strongly disagree	L – limited
VSD – very strongly disagree	VL – very limited

1. The technology (processes) employed in our operation are significantly superior to that of others in the industry.

   VSA_____ SA_____ SLA_____ SDA_____ SD_____ VSD_____

2. Few substitutes exist for our output.

   VSA_____ SA_____ SLA_____ SDA_____ SD_____ VSD_____

3. Our performance is closely monitored by HQ.

   VSA_____ SA_____ SLA_____ SDA_____ SD_____ VSD_____

4. Our managerial know-how is superior to that of other corporations.

   VSA_____ SA_____ SLA_____ SDA_____ SD_____ VSD_____

5. HQ expects periodic written reports on (profit and loss statement, production figures, sales figures, etc.) all aspects of our operations.

   VSA_____ SA_____ SLA_____ SDA_____ SD_____ VSD_____

6. Reactions to changes in the environment are made only after careful deliberation.

   VSA_____ SA_____ SLA_____ SDA_____ SD_____ VSD_____

7. If we had the option we would rather be supplying the U.S. markets through exports than manufacturing here.

   VSA_____ SA_____ SLA_____ SDA_____ SD_____ VSD_____

SCALE KEY

Agree-Disagree Scale	Influence Scale
VSA – very strongly agree	VC – very considerable
SA – strongly agree	C – considerable
SLA – slightly agree	FC – fairly considerable
SDA – slightly disagree	FL – fairly limited
SD – strongly disagree	L – limited
VSD – very strongly disagree	VL – very limited

8. The influence exercised by corporate headquarters in determining our raw material input sources is

    VC_____ C_____ FC_____ FL_____ L_____ VL_____

9. A large number of consumers will be adversely affected if we cease our operations.

    VSA_____ SA_____ SLA_____ SDA_____ SD_____ VSD_____

10. Our operations are basic to the health of the economy.

    VSA_____ SA_____ SLA_____ SDA_____ SD_____ VSD_____

11. The impact of our imports on the U.S. Balance of Trade position is

    VC_____ C_____ FC_____ FL_____ L_____ VL_____

12. It may be necessary for a company to cope with a hostile environment by adopting a low profile.

    VSA_____ SA_____ SLA_____ SDA_____ SD_____ VSD_____

13. The influence exercised by corporate headquarters in determining our sources of capital is

    VC_____ C_____ FC_____ FL_____ L_____ VL_____

14. Favorable labor conditions in the U.S. figured prominently in our decision to invest here.

    VSA_____ SA_____ SLA_____ SDA_____ SD_____ VSD_____

15. Currently our basic strategy is to get the best return on our investment as we do not contemplate operating in the U.S. for any substantial length of time.

    VSA_____ SA_____ SLA_____ SDA_____ SD_____ VSD_____

SCALE KEY

Agree-Disagree Scale	Influence Scale
VSA – very strongly agree	VC – very considerable
SA – strongly agree	C – considerable
SLA – slightly agree	FC – fairly considerable
SDA – slightly disagree	FL – fairly limited
SD – strongly disagree	L – limited
VSD – very strongly disagree	VL – very limited

16. We believe that any decision taken by subsidiary management should benefit our organization as a whole and not benefit either home or host country constituencies exclusively.

VSA_____ SA_____ SLA_____ SDA_____ SD_____ VSD_____

17. A major factor in our investment decision was that we saw the U.S. as being a safe haven for capital for many years to come.

VSA_____ SA_____ SLA_____ SDA_____ SD_____ VSD_____

18. A large number of U.S. firms depend on us to purchase their output.

VSA_____ SA_____ SLA_____ SDA_____ SD_____ VSD_____

19. One of the strategy options that we keep open for our subsidiary is mergers with other companies.

VSA_____ SA_____ SLA_____ SDA_____ SD_____ VSD_____

20. Our processes/products are protected by patents.

VSA_____ SA_____ SLA_____ SDA_____ SD_____ VSD_____

21. Intensity of competition is very low for most of our products/ services.

VSA_____ SA_____ SLA_____ SDA_____ SD_____ VSD_____

22. Long term we see substantial expansion of our activities through vertical integration.

VSA_____ SA_____ SLA_____ SDA_____ SD_____ VSD_____

23. The influence exercised by corporate headquarters in determining the products/services we offer is

VC_____ C_____ FC_____ FL_____ L_____ VL_____

SCALE KEY

Agree-Disagree Scale	Influence Scale
VSA - very strongly agree	VC - very considerable
SA - strongly agree	C - considerable
SLA - slightly agree	FC - fairly considerable
SDA - slightly disagree	FL - fairly limited
SD - strongly disagree	L - limited
VSD - very strongly disagree	VL - very limited

24. A major consideration in our investment decisions was to take advantage of investment incentives that were offered to us.

   VSA_____ SA_____ SLA_____ SDA_____ SD_____ VSD_____

25. Important policy decisions concerning our subsidiary are made by us and ratified by HQ.

   VSA_____ SA_____ SLA_____ SDA_____ SD_____ VSD_____

26. Our products/services are significantly different from those offered by competition.

   VSA_____ SA_____ SLA_____ SDA_____ SD_____ VSD_____

27. Short-term profits may have to be traded for ensuring long-term growth.

   VSA_____ SA_____ SLA_____ SDA_____ SD_____ VSD_____

28. Written manuals exist for almost all key functions.

   VSA_____ SA_____ SLA_____ SDA_____ SD_____ VSD_____

29. Our subsidiary contributes a significant percentage of the sales of the total organization.

   VSA_____ SA_____ SLA_____ SDA_____ SD_____ VSD_____

30. We believe that decisions made by subsidiary management should best reflect the interests of the host country (U.S.).

   VSA_____ SA_____ SLA_____ SDA_____ SD_____ VSD_____

31. The influence exercised by corporate headquarters on our capital investment decisions is

   VC_____ C_____ FC_____ FL_____ L_____ VL_____

SCALE KEY

Agree-Disagree Scale	Influence Scale
VSA - very strongly agree	VC - very considerable
SA - strongly agree	C - considerable
SLA - slightly agree	FC - fairly considerable
SDA - slightly disagree	FL - fairly limited
SD - strongly disagree	L - limited
VSD - very strongly disagree	VL - very limited

32. A large number of domestic firms depend on us to provide critical inputs for their operations.

    VSA_____ SA_____ SLA_____ SDA_____ SD_____ VSD_____

33. Corporate headquarters expect us to conform to written policies for decision making.

    VSA_____ SA_____ SLA_____ SDA_____ SD_____ VSD_____

34. We are a key subsidiary in plans for the long-term growth and development of the total organization.

    VSA_____ SA_____ SLA_____ SDA_____ SD_____ VSD_____

35. If our operations were discontinued, implications for the U.S. economy (employment, critical products and services, etc.) would be significant.

    VSA_____ SA_____ SLA_____ SDA_____ SD_____ VSD_____

36. Our organization is a key entity in the marketing and distribution channels of the total organization (parent and all subsidiaries and affiliates).

    VSA_____ SA_____ SLA_____ SDA_____ SD_____ VSD_____

37. Important policy decisions concerning our subsidiary are jointly determined by HQ and subsidiary management.

    VSA_____ SA_____ SLA_____ SDA_____ SD_____ VSD_____

38. The influence exercised by corporate headquarters in the selection of top management level personnel is

    VC_____ C_____ FC_____ FL_____ L_____ VL_____

SCALE KEY

Agree-Disagree Scale	Influence Scale
VSA – very strongly agree	VC – very considerable
SA – strongly agree	C – considerable
SLA – slightly agree	FC – fairly considerable
SDA – slightly disagree	FL – fairly limited
SD – strongly disagree	L – limited
VSD – very strongly disagree	VL – very limited

39. We make key decisions primarily on the basis of the effect they would have on the performance of our subsidiary.

    VSA_____ SA_____ SLA_____ SDA_____ SD_____ VSD_____

40. A significant percentage of the profits of the total organization is generated by us.

    VSA_____ SA_____ SLA_____ SDA_____ SD_____ VSD_____

41. Our investment in the U.S. was a direct result of investments made in the U.S. by our major domestic (home) competitor.

    VSA_____ SA_____ SLA_____ SDA_____ SD_____ VSD_____

42. Long term we see a substantial expansion in the range of products/services we manufacture (offer) here in the U.S.

    VSA_____ SA_____ SLA_____ SDA_____ SD_____ VSD_____

43. The influence exercised by corporate headquarters in subsidiary marketing decisions is

    VC_____ C_____ FC_____ FL_____ L_____ VL_____

44. Long term we see a significant expansion of our activities in this country through acquisition of existing companies.

    VSA_____ SA_____ SLA_____ SDA_____ SD_____ VSD_____

45. Our operations have a significant impact on the economic well-being of the state/region in which we operate.

    VSA_____ SA_____ SLA_____ SDA_____ SD_____ VSD_____

46. Our subsidiary provides critical inputs to the parent as well as other subsidiaries and affiliates.

    VSA_____ SA_____ SLA_____ SDA_____ SD_____ VSD_____

SCALE KEY

Agree–Disagree Scale	Influence Scale
VSA – very strongly agree	VC – very considerable
SA – strongly agree	C – considerable
SLA – slightly agree	FC – fairly considerable
SDA – slightly disagree	FL – fairly limited
SD – strongly disagree	L – limited
VSD – very strongly disagree	VL – very limited

47. Our exports have a significant impact on the U.S. balance of trade position.

    VSA_____ SA_____ SLA_____ SDA_____ SD_____ VSD_____

48. The influence exercised by corporate headquarters in selecting our middle/lower management personnel is

    VC_____ C_____ FC_____ FL_____ L_____ VL_____

49. Important policy decisions concerning our subsidiary are determined by HQ and implemented by us.

    VSA_____ SA_____ SLA_____ SDA_____ SD_____ VSD_____

50. All our long-term plans are geared toward maintaining our status quo in the market.

    VSA_____ SA_____ SLA_____ SDA_____ SD_____ VSD_____

51. A substantial proportion of our inputs is obtained from the parent and/or other subsidiaries and affiliates.

    VSA_____ SA_____ SLA_____ SDA_____ SD_____ VSD_____

52. Only a very limited number of alternatives exist for our technical know-how.

    VSA_____ SA_____ SLA_____ SDA_____ SD_____ VSD_____

53. With regard to policy decisions affecting our operations, the influence we exercise is

    VC_____ C_____ FC_____ FL_____ L_____ VL_____

54. We believe that decisions made by subsidiary management should best reflect the interests of the home (parent) country.

    VSA_____ SA_____ SLA_____ SDA_____ SD_____ VSD_____

SCALE KEY

Agree-Disagree Scale	Influence Scale
VSA - very strongly agree	VC - very considerable
SA - strongly agree	C - considerable
SLA - slightly agree	FC - fairly considerable
SDA - slightly disagree	FL - fairly limited
SD - strongly disagree	L - limited
VSD - very strongly disagree	VL - very limited

55. The influence exercised by corporate headquarters in determining our aggregate production schedule is

   VC_____ C_____ FC_____ FL_____ L_____ VL_____

56. We contribute significantly to the R & D function of the total organization.

   VSA_____ SA_____ SLA_____ SDA_____ SD_____ VSD_____

57. Only a very limited number of alternatives exist for our managerial know-how.

   VSA_____ SA_____ SLA_____ SDA_____ SD_____ VSD_____

58. The degree of autonomy we have in running our operations is

   VC_____ C_____ FC_____ FL_____ L_____ VL_____

59. An aggressive policy is the best policy to adopt when dealing with members of a hostile environment as it puts them on the defensive.

   VSA_____ SA_____ SLA_____ SDA_____ SD_____ VSD_____

60. An important consideration in our investment decision was to utilize some competitive advantage (technology, patent, etc.) that we possessed.

   VSA_____ SA_____ SLA_____ SDA_____ SD_____ VSD_____

61. HQ management believes short-term performance is more important than long-term viability.

   VSA_____ SA_____ SLA_____ SDA_____ SD_____ VSD_____

SCALE KEY

Agree-Disagree Scale	Influence Scale
VSA – very strongly agree	VC – very considerable
SA – strongly agree	C – considerable
SLA – slightly agree	FC – fairly considerable
SDA – slightly disagree	FL – fairly limited
SD – strongly disagree	L – limited
VSD – very strongly disagree	VL – very limited

62. An important consideration in our investment decision was to prevent competition from pre-empting the market.

    VSA_____ SA_____ SLA_____ SDA_____ SD_____ VSD_____

63. Maintaining good relations with significant members of the environment (government officials, politicians, etc.) is critical to our effectiveness.

    VSA_____ SA_____ SLA_____ SDA_____ SD_____ VSD_____

64. Our investment would constitute a significant part of the total capital investment in the country.

    VSA_____ SA_____ SLA_____ SDA_____ SD_____ VSD_____

65. Layoffs, if made, are utilized only as the very last resort.

    VSA_____ SA_____ SLA_____ SDA_____ SD_____ VSD_____

66. Information is widely dispersed within the organization.

    VSA_____ SA_____ SLA_____ SDA_____ SD_____ VSD_____

67. Expatriates are instructed to avoid close and visible association with each other in the host country.

    VSA_____ SA_____ SLA_____ SDA_____ SD_____ VSD_____

68. In many situations, it may be necessary to act rather than wait to obtain complete information.

    VSA_____ SA_____ SLA_____ SDA_____ SD_____ VSD_____

69. Bottom up initiatives are strongly encouraged.

    VSA_____ SA_____ SLA_____ SDA_____ SD_____ VSD_____

SCALE KEY

Agree-Disagree Scale	Influence Scale
VSA - very strongly agree	VC - very considerable
SA - strongly agree	C - considerable
SLA - slightly agree	FC - fairly considerable
SDA - slightly disagree	FL - fairly limited
SD - strongly disagree	L - limited
VSD - very strongly disagree	VL - very limited

70. Our investment would constitute a significant part of the total capital investment in the immediate economic region (county, state).

    VSA_____ SA_____ SLA_____ SDA_____ SD_____ VSD_____

71. Management is greatly concerned with the welfare of the community in which it operates.

    VSA_____ SA_____ SLA_____ SDA_____ SD_____ VSD_____

72. The chief executive has to take responsibility for the performance of the organization.

    VSA_____ SA_____ SLA_____ SDA_____ SD_____ VSD_____

73. Conscious efforts are made to minimize the status differentials between employees and management.

    VSA_____ SA_____ SLA_____ SDA_____ SD_____ VSD_____

74. Interactions are kept as informal as possible.

    VSA_____ SA_____ SLA_____ SDA_____ SD_____ VSD_____

75. Our investment contributes significantly to the total level of employment in the country.

    VSA_____ SA_____ SLA_____ SDA_____ SD_____ VSD_____

76. A marked preference for the consensus mode is demonstrated in decision making.

    VSA_____ SA_____ SLA_____ SDA_____ SD_____ VSD_____

77. Management is greatly concerned with the welfare of employees.

    VSA_____ SA_____ SLA_____ SDA_____ SD_____ VSD_____

SCALE KEY

Agree-Disagree Scale	Influence Scale
VSA - very strongly agree	VC - very considerable
SA - strongly agree	C - considerable
SLA - slightly agree	FC - fairly considerable
SDA - slightly disagree	FL - fairly limited
SD - strongly disagree	L - limited
VSD - very strongly disagree	VL - very limited

78. A long-term perspective is essential for the evaluation of key decisions.

   VSA_____ SA_____ SLA_____ SDA_____ SD_____ VSD_____

79. Our investment contributes significantly to the total employment in the immediate economic region.

   VSA_____ SA_____ SLA_____ SDA_____ SD_____ VSD_____

80. Humanism takes precedence over economics.

   VSA_____ SA_____ SLA_____ SDA_____ SD_____ VSD_____

81. Group emphasis is greater than individual emphasis.

   VSA_____ SA_____ SLA_____ SDA_____ SD_____ VSD_____

82. Conscious efforts are made to interact socially with the community in which our operations are located.

   VSA_____ SA_____ SLA_____ SDA_____ SD_____ VSD_____

83. Middle management is viewed as being the key resource for problem identification and solution.

   VSA_____ SA_____ SLA_____ SDA_____ SD_____ VSD_____

84. We operate under the maxim 'When in Rome do as Romans do.'

   VSA_____ SA_____ SLA_____ SDA_____ SD_____ VSD_____

85. Responsibility for company performance has to be shared by top management of the company.

   VSA_____ SA_____ SLA_____ SDA_____ SD_____ VSD_____

SCALE KEY

Agree-Disagree Scale	Influence Scale
VSA - very strongly agree	VC - very considerable
SA - strongly agree	C - considerable
SLA - slightly agree	FC - fairly considerable
SDA - slightly disagree	FL - fairly limited
SD - strongly disagree	L - limited
VSD - very strongly disagree	VL - very limited

86. Top management is viewed as a facilitator of information than an issuer of edicts.

    VSA_____ SA_____ SLA_____ SDA_____ SD_____ VSD_____

87. Lateral communication is the preferred communication mode.

    VSA_____ SA_____ SLA_____ SDA_____ SD_____ VSD_____

88. Management is equally concerned with process/technological resources as it is with people.

    VSA_____ SA_____ SLA_____ SDA_____ SD_____ VSD_____

89. A marked preference for the concensus mode is demonstrated in decision making.

    VSA_____ SA_____ SLA_____ SDA_____ SD_____ VSD_____

Top management is viewed as a facilitator of information rather than an issuer of edicts.

Appendix C

Interview Guide for the
Study in the Developing Countries

Interview Guide

A STUDY OF MULTINATIONAL CORPORATIONS

This section contains questions related to the attributes of your
company. Please answer them as indicated. The data would primarily
be used for classificatory purposes. Please do not indicate either
your name and designation or the name of the corporation in which
you are employed:

SECTION 1

I.   Country in which the company operates: _____
      (Host Country)

II.   Country in which the controlling ownership resides: _____
      (Home Country)

III. Your company is: (Please Check)

      [____] (a) Wholly owned by the parent

      [____] (b) Joint venture with host country entrepreneur

                 [____] (1) majority equity holding by parent

                 [____] (2) minority equity holding by parent

      [____] (c) Joint venture with host government

                 [____] (1) majority equity holding by parent

                 [____] (2) minority equity holding by parent

      [____] (d) Any other (please specify)

                 _____

                 _____

                 _____

V.   INDUSTRY IN WHICH A LARGE PROPORTION OF THE FIRM'S ACTIVITIES ARE
      CONCENTRATED: (please check)

      [____] (a) petrochemicals

      [____] (b) pharmaceutical

      [____] (c) mining/crude extraction

[ ] (d) general manufacturing/fabrication

[ ] (e) automobiles

[ ] (f) rubber tires

[ ] (g) consumer durables

[ ] (h) consumer non-durables

[ ] (i) foods, agricultural business

[ ] (j) textiles

[ ] (k) trading

[ ] (l) any other (please specify) _____

VI. SIZE:

    (a) Capital investment: _____ Currency specified: _____
    (b) Sales volume: _____ Currency specified: _____
    (c) Number of employees: _____

VII. What is your perception of the scale of your operations with reference to other corporations operating in the country? (please check)

[ ] (a) Very large

[ ] (b) Large

[ ] (c) Medium

[ ] (d) Small

VIII. AGE
How long has your company been operating in this country?
(a) _____ number of years

IX. With reference to other companies operating in the country, what level of technology does your company utilize in its primary operations? (please check)

[ ] (a) Advanced technology

[ ] (b) Intermediate technology

[ ] (c) Low, unsophisticated technology

X. DIVERSIFICATION:

How many <u>distinct</u> products and/or services does your company offer? (please check)

(a) _____ products
(c) _____ services

XI. PERSONNEL DATA:

What percentage of your personnel, at various levels of the organization, are:

(a) nationals from the MNC's home country?
(b) nationals of the host country?
(c) nationals of a third country?

Levels	(a)	(b)	(c)
(1) top level	___%	___%	___%
(2) second level	___%	___%	___%
(3) third level	___%	___%	___%
(4) fourth level	___%	___%	___%

XII. MARKET ORIENTATION

Listed below are a set of statements concerning the distribution of your company's products. Please check the one that is most appropriate for the majority of your company's products.

☐ (a) Majority of the output is sold to the parent and/or subsidiaries of the parent.

☐ (b) Majority of output sold to consumers in the home country.

☐ (c) Majority of output sold to consumers in third countries.

☐ (d) Majority of output sold to consumers in the host country.

☐ (e) Majority of output sold to governmental agencies in the host country.

XIII. (a) What is the approximate market share held by your primary products/services? ____%

(b) Please indicate the extent of backlog of orders faced by your main products/services over the past year.

1 ... 2 ... 3 ... 4 ... 5 ... 6 ... 7
large   moderate   no
backlog   backlog   backlog

(c) Please indicate the degree of competition faced by your organization for its major products and/or services.

$$1 \ldots 2 \ldots 3 \ldots 4 \ldots 5 \ldots 6 \ldots 7$$

intense	moderate	no
competition	competition	competition

(d) <u>Overall</u>, would you rate the market for your major products and/or services as: (please check)

(a) Seller's market
(b) Moderately competitive market
(c) Highly competitive market

Below are listed a number of possible expectations host governments can have of MNCs. Please consider each separately and respond, in the respective columns, to questions asked about them.

Expectation	Employing the scale below, please indicate how strong your company feels this expectation to be to the host government 1 2 3 4 5 6 7 v. strong mod. v. weak	Employing the scale below, please indicate how precise your host has been with you regarding this expectation 1 2 3 4 5 6 7 v. diff. m. prec. v. prec.	Employing the scale below, please estimate the magnitude of impact on the host your firm has had 1 2 3 4 5 6 7 v. sig. mod. v. low
1. Providing capital inflow from sources outside the host.	—	—	—
2. Providing skilled manpower from sources outside the host.	—	—	—
3. Providing useful technology which would not otherwise be used here from outside the host country.	—	—	—
4. Providing additional entrepreneurial spirit to the host country's people.	—	—	—
5. Introducing new R & D efforts that would not otherwise be attempted in this country.	—	—	—
6. Providing raw materials which would not otherwise be available here from outside (other countries).	—	—	—
7. Creating a positive balance of payments position through capital inflows, new exports, reducing imports etc.	—	—	—
8. Assisting local entrepreneurs in increasing their share of the enterprise, i.e., increasing local ownership.	—	—	—

145

Below are listed a number of possible expectations host governments can have of MNCs. Please consider each separately and respond, in the respective columns, to questions asked about them.

Expectation	Employing the scale below, please indicate how strong your company feels this expectation to be to the host government	Employing the scale below, please indicate how precise your host has been with you regarding this expectation	Employing the scale below, please estimate the magnitude of impact on the host your firm has had
	1 2 3 4 5 6 7 v. strong mod. v. weak	1 2 3 4 5 6 7 v. diff. m. prec. v. prec.	1 2 3 4 5 6 7 v. sig. mod. v. low
9. Expanding credit facilities for local customers by making it available to them.	—	—	—
10. Increasing competitive (antimonopolistic) tendencies in local markets.	—	—	—
11. Not displacing local investors or local enterprise investment.	—	—	—
12. Developing local resources more fully.	—	—	—
13. Upgrading the wages generally paid in your economic sector.	—	—	—
14. Using local suppliers for factor inputs.	—	—	—
15. Increasing the stability of the local economy.	—	—	—
16. Demonstrating good corporate citizenship by not disturbing social and cultural values.	—	—	—
17. Introducing new "mass goods" into the economy which would otherwise not have been introduced.	—	—	—

146

Below are listed a number of possible expectations host governments can have of MNCs. Please consider each separately and respond, in the respective columns, to questions asked about them.

Expectation	Employing the scale below, please indicate how strong your company feels this expectation to be to the host government 1 2 3 4 5 6 7 v. strong mod. v. weak	Employing the scale below, please indicate how precise your host has been with you regarding this expectation 1 2 3 4 5 6 7 v. diff. m. prec. v. prec.	Employing the scale below, please estimate the magnitude of impact on the host your firm has had 1 2 3 4 5 6 7 v. sig. mod. v. low
18. Stimulating desire for socio economic growth.	—	—	—
19. Increasing employment at all levels.	—	—	—
20. Upgrading the nature of employment, especially skilled employment.	—	—	—
21. Increasing the participation of workers in decision making.	—	—	—
22. Expanding the awareness of local workers to a wider range of employment possibilities.	—	—	—
23. Increasing the variety of goods for local consumer purchase.	—	—	—
24. Increasing the quality of goods for local consumer purchase.	—	—	—
25. Increasing the variety of services available for local consumers.	—	—	—
26. Creating lower prices for locally sold goods and services.	—	—	—

147

Below are listed a number of possible expectations host governments can have of MNCs. Please consider each separately and respond, in the respective columns, to questions asked about them.

Expectation	Employing the scale below, please indicate how strong your company feels this expectation to be to the host government	Employing the scale below, please indicate how precise your host has been with you regarding this expectation	Employing the scale below, please estimate the magnitude of impact on the host your firm has had
	1 2 3 4 5 6 7 v. strong mod. v. weak	1 2 3 4 5 6 7 v. diff. m. prec. v. prec.	1 2 3 4 5 6 7 v. sig. mod. v. low
27. Increasing availability of repair and service facilities.	–	–	–
28. Providing education for local customers regarding new products and services.	–	–	–

148

Section 3

Listed below are a number of possible expectations that the MNCs can have of the host government. Please consider each separately and respond in the margins to the questions asked about them.

Expectation	Using the scale below, please respond to the question: WITH WHAT DEGREE OF INTENSITY DO YOU DESIRE THE HOST GOVERNMENT MEET THESE EXPECTATIONS?	Using the scale below, please respond to the question: HOW CLEARLY HAVE YOU MADE THESE EXPECTATIONS KNOWN TO THE HOST GOVERNMENT?
	1 2 3 4 5 6 7 strong mod. mild desire desire desire	1 2 3 4 5 6 7 diffuse mod. very precise precise
1. The host government should provide the necessary infrastructure.	—	—
2. The host government should reduce bureaucratic controls.	—	—
3. The host government should not interfere with the affairs of the corporation.	—	—
4. The host government should provide conducive labor legislation.	—	—
5. The host government should provide conducive business government relationship.	—	—

6. The host government should permit more flexible expansion and diversification.

7. The host government should not exercise a high degree of control on remittances of dividends or fees to the parent.

8. The host government should not insist on dilution of control.

9. The host government should not apply price controls to MNC-products/services.

10. The host government should spell out clearly all the terms of entry and not make ad hoc changes from time to time.

SECTION 4

I. On the scale below, please indicate the extent to which your corporation finds itself in conflict with the host government, or other
organizations in the host country.

    1 ... 2 ... 3 ... 4 ... 5 ... 6 ... 7
    always   sometimes   never

If your corporation has had conflicts with host government or other
organizations, please recall the two most recent conflicts, and respond
to the following set of questions as indicated.

SECTION 4a

I. Could you briefly describe the first conflict.

_____
_____
_____
_____

II. On the scale below, please indicate the intensity of the conflict
described above.

    1 ... 2 ... 3 ... 4 ... 5 ... 6 ... 7
    high   moderate   low
    intensity   intensity   intensity

III. Below are listed some descriptive categories of the activities
that could follow as a result of the conflict. Please check
those activities that resulted as a consequence of the conflict.
You may check more than one.

☐ (a) Calling of names

☐ (b) Personal attacks

☐ (c) Public debate

☐ (d) Newspaper headlines

☐ (e) Parliamentary discussion

☐ (f) Discussion at the association/group level

☐ (g) The two parties involved discuss the issues separately
       after having been unable to resolve it together, i.e.,
       no one is listening to the other.

☐ (h) Parliamentary debate where both parties, as well as a third independent group--academicians, etc.--are invited to participate

☐ (i) Only scholarly discussion; not much of a public issue

☐ (j) The individual conflict is resolved without much fuss

IV. In the following set, please check the members of the MNC who were involved in the conflict.

☐ (a) <u>Home</u> office executives.

☐ (b) Chief executive of subsidiary.

☐ (c) Functional/operating managers of the subsidiary.

V. In the following, please check the representatives of the host country/government who were involved in the conflict.

☐ (a) Cabinet members

☐ (b) High-level civil service personnel

☐ (c) Heads of agencies and lower-level personnel

☐ (d) Organizational heads (e.g., labor leaders)

VI. (a) If any government agencies or other members of the environment (employee unions, suppliers, distributors, etc.) were involved, please indicate the number of such constituencies involved. (please check)

☐ (1) more than 4 agencies

☐ (2) 2, 3 agencies

☐ (3) one agency

(b) In the set below, please indicate the constituencies involved in the conflict (you may check more than one).

☐ (1) employees and their representatives

☐ (2) suppliers

☐ (3) distributors

☐ (4) consumers and their representatives

☐ (5) utilities

[   ] (6) local government representatives

[   ] (7) other _____ (please supply)

VII. Please indicate on the following scale the consequences (to your company) of the conflict you just described.

```
    1  ... 2  ... 3  ... 4  ... 5  ... 6  ... 7
  complete  const.      high      minor      no
  breakdown residual    level     headaches  impact
  in rela-  problems    of
  tionship              frustration
```

VIII. Please indicate on the following scale the spillover impact of this conflict on other MNCs operating here.

```
    1 ... 2 ... 3 ... 4 ... 5 ... 6 ... 7
  considerable     moderate          no
    impact          impact          impact
```

IX. Please indicate on the following scale the spillover impact of this conflict on <u>your</u> operations in <u>other</u> countries.

```
    1 ... 2 ... 3 ... 4 ... 5 ... 6 ... 7
  considerable     moderate          no
    impact          impact          impact
```

X. Please indicate on the following scale the spillover impact of this conflict on the operations of <u>other MNCs</u> in <u>other</u> countries.

```
    1 ... 2 ... 3 ... 4 ... 5 ... 6 ... 7
  considerable     moderate          no
    impact          impact          impact
```

SECTION 4b

THE QUESTIONS IN THIS SECTION ARE <u>EXACTLY</u> IDENTICAL TO THOSE IN SECTION 4a. THIS SECTION WAS DESIGNED TO OBTAIN DETAILS PERTAINING TO THE SECOND CONFLICT.

SECTION 5

I. As a result of the conflicts that you described, has your corporation made any changes in your strategy of dealing with the host government or other organizations?

_____
_____
_____
_____

II. Can you identify any changes that the host government/other organization has made in its strategy in dealing with you as a reult of the conflict? (please explain)

_____
_____
_____
_____

III. What general changes in attitude, that will have an impact on your operations, have you noticed on the part of the host government or other organizations?

_____
_____
_____
_____

SECTION 6

I. Below are listed ten kinds of controls host governments have imposed on MNCs. Using the scale provided, please indicate your estimate of the percentage probability that each control will be instituted for you (if not used now) or strengthened (if already used) by your host within the coming five years.

```
    1  ... 2 ... 3 ... 4 ... 5 ... 6 ... 7 ... 8 ... 9
less than 11-  21-  31-  41-  51-  61-  71-  more than
        10%  20%  30%  40%  50%  60%  70%  80%  90%
```

(a) Requiring foreign firms to share ownership with nationals.

(b) Requiring that specified proportions of key positions in executive ranks or on boards be filled with nationals.

(c) Placing ceiling rates on royalties and/or fees paid to the parent firm, or disallowing parent firms from collecting licensing fees from affiliates.

(d) Removing foreign participation from technologically stagnant industries.

(e) Renegotiating concession contracts and making them more favorable to local interests.

(f) Insisting that foreign firms raise more capital outside the host's financial markets rather than competing with national interests.

(g) Pressuring foreign firms to engage in broader and more intensive training programs for nationals.

(h) Increasing local content requirements in foreign firm's output.

(i) Pressuring foreign firms to develop/expand export markets.

(j) Pressuring foreign firms to rely less on parent-home government in disputes with the host government.

II. Please indicate on the scale below the likely impact of the host government's regulatory actions over the next five years on the operations of your corporation.

```
            1 ... 2 ... 3 ... 4 ... 5 ... 6 ... 7
        greatly decrease          no        greatly increase
    management flexibility      impact    management flexibility
        over operations                       over operations
```

III. Please indicate on the scale below the likely impact of the host government's regulatory actions over the next five years on your ability to practice international specialization.

```
            1 ... 2 ... 3 ... 4 ... 5 ... 6 ... 7
        greatly increase          no        greatly decrease
    ability to specialize       impact    ability to specialize
        internationally                       internationally
```

SECTION 7

I.   On the scale below, please indicate the general state of <u>home-host relationship</u> over the past five years.

```
            1 ... 2 ... 3 ... 4 ... 5 ... 6 ... 7
           very        business-              volatile
          cordial         like              and hostile
```

II. As a policy (or <u>de facto</u>) does your firm feel a responsibility to: (please check)

- [ ] (a) agree publicly and act in accordance with the foreign and domestic policies of the host government.

- [ ] (b) agree publicly and act in accordance with the foreign and domestic policies of the home country.

- [ ] (c) stay free from public identification with the policies of either country.

III. Does the general state of the home-host relationship affect your company's policy in any meaningful way?

$$1 \ldots 2 \ldots 3 \ldots 4 \ldots 5 \ldots 6 \ldots 7$$

| great impact | moderate impact | no impact |

IV. In your judgment, have any of the conflicts you described come directly or indirectly from problems that your home country and your host country have experienced diplomatically? (please check)

☐ (a) yes

☐ (b) no

If yes, please explain: _____

_____

_____

V. To the best of your knowledge, have any of the conflicts you have had with your host government <u>caused</u> diplomatic problems between your home country and your host? (please check)

☐ (a) yes

☐ (b) no

If yes, please explain: _____

_____

_____

VI. a) With what official in the host country does your corporation regularly deal? (please check)

☐ (a) Cabinet minister

☐ (b) High-level civil service personnel

☐ (c) Heads of government agencies

☐ (d) Other, please specify. _____

b) What is the nature of this relationship? (please indicate)

$$1 \ldots 2 \ldots 3 \ldots 4 \ldots 5 \ldots 6 \ldots 7$$

| very cordial | business-like | cool/hostile |

VII. Which corporate official has the responsibility to maintain this relationship with the host? (please check)

☐ (a) Managing director

☐ (b) President/chief executive

☐ (c) Functional managers

☐ (d) Other, please specify _____

What special talents does he need to have to do this job effectively? (please check)

☐ (a) Interpersonal competence

☐ (b) Influential contacts

☐ (c) Political ability and sensitivity

☐ (d) Other, please specify _____

VIII. Do you use someone from "outside" your firm to work on behalf of your company to deal with the host government? (please check)

☐ (a) yes

☐ (b) no

If yes, whom: _____

Why: _____
_____
_____

IX. In general, how helpful is the foreign office (or are other home government agencies) in helping you to deal with the host?

```
        1 ... 2 ... 3 ... 4 ... 5 ... 6 ... 7
        very           moderately         of no
        helpful         helpful        help at all
```

X. On the scale below, please indicate what you see as the future for your corporation in this country?

```
        1 ... 2 ... 3 ... 4 ... 5 ... 6 ... 7
   unconditionally    moderately      unconditionally
        good            good               bad
```

XI. On the scale below, please indicate what you see as the future for all MNCs operating in this country?

```
        1 ... 2 ... 3 ... 4 ... 5 ... 6 ... 7
   unconditionally    moderately      unconditionally
        good            good               bad
```

XII. If you had known all the problems associated with operating here, would you have invested?

        1 ... 2 ... 3 ... 4 ... 5 ... 6 ... 7
   invested without   invested with   not at all
    reservations   reservations

XIII. Do you plan to expand your operations here given your present commitments?

        1 ... 2 ... 3 ... 4 ... 5 ... 6 ... 7
   expand without   expand with   not at all
    reservations   reservations

XIV. Have you been given any preferential treatment by your host government over others on any substantive matter?

   [   ] (a) yes

   [   ] (b) no

If yes, please explain: _____

_____

XV. Have others, nationals or MNCs, been given prefential treatment over your firm on any substantive matters?

   [   ] (a) yes

   [   ] (b) yes

If yes, please explain: _____

_____

SECTION 8

The accomplishment or non-accomplishment of the following list of potential contributions an MNC can make to a host country has been used as an argument for and against MNCs by businessmen, union leaders, and politicians. Under each of these categories, please indicate what specific steps your company has taken toward their attainment.

(a) transferring advanced managerial expertise.

_____

(b) transferring technological expertise.

_____

(c) research and development transfer.

_____

(d)   increasing host country's exports.

_____

(e)   decreasing host country's imports.

_____

(f)   providing significant employment to nationals.

_____

(g)   acting as accelerator for the host country's industrial growth.

_____

(h)   providing example of good corporate behavior.

_____

Name Index

Subject Index

About the Authors

Anant R. Negandhi is Professor of International Business at the University of Illinois at Urbana-Champaign. He earned his B.A. and B. Com. degrees from the University of Bombay, his M.B.A. from Texas Christian University, and his Ph.D. from Michigan State University. Prior to joining the University of Illinois faculty, Dr. Negandhi taught at the University of California at Los Angeles and at Kent State University. During 1976–1978, he served as Senior Research Fellow at the International Institute of Management, Science Center Berlin. In 1977 he was appointed a fellow of the Academy of Management and, in 1971, and Outstanding Educator of America. Dr. Negandhi has published over sixty scholarly articles in various journals. He is the author, coauthor, or editor of numerous books; two of the most recent are *Quest for Survival and Growth: A Comparative Study of American, European, and Japanese Multinationals* (1979) and *The Functioning of Complex Organizations* (1981). In addition, he was founder-editor of the quarterly journal *Organization and Administrative Sciences*.

B. R. Baliga, who received his D.B.A. from Kent State University, is Assistant Professor of International Business and Business Policy at Texas Tech University. He is the coauthor of *Quest for Survival and Growth: A Comparative Study of American, European, and Japanese Multinationals*.

About the
Science Center Berlin

The Wissenschaftszentrum Berlin (Science Center Berlin), a non-profit corporation, serves as a parent institution for institutes conducting social science research in areas of significant social concern.

The following institutes are currently operating within the Science Center Berlin:

1. The International Institute of Management,
2. The International Institute for Environment and Society,
3. The International Institute for Comparative Social Research.

They share the following structural elements: a multinational professional and supporting staff, multidisciplinary project teams, a focus on international comparative studies, a policy orientation in the selection of research topics and the diffusion of results.